Life on the Deben

The Story of a Suffolk River

Nick Cottam and Tim Curtis

Life on the Deben

The Story of a Suffolk River

Nick Cottam and Tim Curtis

Published in the UK by LoTD Publishing

lifeonthedeben.com

ISBN 978-1-5272-4971-4

Printed and bound by Fuller Davies Printing & Mailing, Ipswich, Suffolk
fullerdavies.co.uk

Contents

Foreword by John McCarthy   8
Introduction   9

Chapter 1   Searching for the source   10
Chapter 2   Downriver from Debenham   16
Chapter 3   Invasion and settlement   28
Chapter 4   A trading river   44
Chapter 5   Adapt and survive   60
Chapter 6   Time and tide   64
Chapter 7   Creative backdrop   72
Chapter 8   On the water   86
Chapter 9   Halfway down   96
Chapter 10   The disappearing village   102
Chapter 11   Saltmarsh and siltation   108
Chapter 12   Wild side   116
Chapter 13   The lost port   122
Chapter 14   We know you're coming   128
Chapter 15   Anyone for a dip?   136
Chapter 16   The harbour master   140
Chapter 17   Protecting the future   144

Deben resources   154
Acknowledgements   155

The entrance to the Deben High water on a serene summer's day. When the tide retreats and the wind blows, the exposed, shifting shingle bar presents a challenge to navigators approaching the river

Debenham

Groaning stone

Brandeston

Kettleburgh

Cretingham

RIVER DEBEN

Easton

Brandeston Ford

Decoy pond

River Alde

Wickham Market

Lower Ufford

Rendlesham

Tide mill

River Ore

Sutton Hoo

Woodbridge

Martlesham

Waldringfield

Goseford (ancient port)

Ramsholt

Hemley

Bawdsey

Felixstowe Ferry

Claudia Myatt

N

7

Foreword

Making the film *Life on the Deben* with Tim Curtis and Malcolm Hodd took two years and was an adventure for all of us. For me, personally, it was a voyage of discovery. Though I had lived in Woodbridge and sailed on the river for many years, I'd never truly appreciated the Deben's importance as an environmental resource and had no idea of its profound historical significance.

I remember sailing my yacht in over the Deben bar, heart pounding as the current swept us terrifyingly close to the seething banks of shingle. With half an eye I noticed families playing peacefully on the beach just a few yards away, blissfully unaware of the drama I was experiencing on the water.

Moments later I was safely in the river, enjoying the tranquil aspect of Bawdsey on one bank and the bustle of Felixstowe Ferry on the other – a grand manor building looking across to a little old fishing village. I knew that Bawdsey Manor had history – it was where radar was developed during the Second World War – but I had no idea that 700 years ago the river mouth was utterly different and formed one of the country's foremost trading ports: Goseford, now vanished.

When I lived in Woodbridge I hardly explored the upper reaches of the Deben, but during filming I saw many beautiful, hidden stretches of the river. One summer's afternoon I sat chatting with the historian Chris Scull in a wide meadow at Rendlesham. As we watched the cows munching on the rich grass, Chris conjured up what had once been there: an Anglo-Saxon royal base, home to Raedwald, almost certainly the first king of England.

The Deben has seen so much. It has inspired writers, musicians, painters and all of us who enjoy walking beside it, or taking to the water to swim, sail and row. Learning about the life of the Deben was a fascinating part of making the film and has contributed to the writing of this book. The river is a delicate natural environment, but with care and commitment it can be preserved for future generations to cherish and enjoy.

John McCarthy, November 2019

Introduction

The Deben is a peaceful river. It emerges quietly from fields and tributaries, flows gently through easy countryside and disappears behind hills and trees, only gathering strength as it broadens to meet its tidal estuary. On occasion, a rainstorm lashes into being a raging torrent. Or, at the river's entrance, a southerly gale battles an ebb tide over the shingle bar to create a maelstrom of white water. But the Deben's key quality is constancy. Its reassuring serenity is a rebuke to a hurried world.

It is a river of two parts: non-tidal in the upper reaches from Debenham to just south of Ufford, and then shaped, emptied and resuscitated by the tide as it passes historic landmarks such as Sutton Hoo, Ramsholt Church and Felixstowe Ferry at the mouth. There, the shifting shingle bar has protected the entrance over the centuries and is still a challenge for navigators today.

The film *Life on the Deben*, on which this book is based, celebrated the beauty and tranquillity of this 25-mile (40km) waterway. Tim Curtis (director), Malcolm Hodd (producer) and the journalist John McCarthy (narrator) used their local knowledge and love of the river to capture its essence.

At its heart, *Life on the Deben* is a community film, based on conversations with people who know, love and make a living from the water. This book salutes the spirit of the film while offering new insights. It is a book about the river's history and commerce, its everyday life and leisure – and, above all, the people who have made and are still making the Deben what it is today.

Chapter 1
Searching for the source

A river runs through it?
John McCarthy walking along a dry Stony Lane in a scene from *Life on the Deben*; inset left is the folkloric Groaning Stone; inset above is Stony Lane all wet in winter

We begin near Debenham. At about two miles long, Stony Lane is reputedly the longest ford in the country. Channelled between steep banks, it can virtually dry up in the summer months, while periods of winter rain can turn the shallow stream into a fast-flowing torrent. It is also touched by folklore: the Groaning Stone, a smooth riverbed rock, is said to turn over and groan at midnight when the moon is full.

Stony Lane adds its own drama to any search for the source of the Deben. It flows or it trickles depending on the time of year, mimicking the ditches and brooks above Debenham that collectively make up the start of a river. "Certainly there is no gushing spring to mark an exact source spot," says Joan Freeman, who, with her husband Peter, farms 800 acres of arable land near the village of Aspall. "The Deben is a bit like a tree trunk, with its upper boughs and branches radiating out [and up] from Debenham."

Any one of those branches might at some time or other lay claim to being the source of the Deben. *Samuel Dove's Debenham*, which was first published in 1839, refers to a stream that in earlier times was much larger – a river. According to old records in the University of Oxford's Bodleian Library, "ships of considerable burthen came up to the Town".

Dove offers up another witness to the idea that big ships were once able to travel so far up the Deben. He writes that "an old person Elizabeth Sharman who died some years since at an advanced age, recollected that an Anchor was found…deeply imbedded in the sands, nearly half a mile above the Town."

Cider country

"By the time my family got here, the Deben was no longer navigable to Debenham," says Henry Chevallier Guild. Henry and his brother Barry are the eighth generation of Chevalliers to have produced the famous Aspall cider since the family moved to the village at the start of the 18th century.

The orchards host one of three Deben catchments in the area, known as the Aspall drains. In heavy rain, water streams off the clay soil, fills up the ditches and drains and rushes down towards Debenham below. Cider leaves more sedately but more noisily, in lorries.

Walk south towards Debenham and you will come across two other Deben catchments: the Derrybrook, which travels down Stony Lane; and Cherry Tree Brook, which emerges at the bottom end of Debenham. Both bring water from the village of Mickfield to the west. All three catchments contribute to the emerging river that enters and leaves Debenham.

Clockwise from top right The Aspall orchards; the original stone wheel and trough, last used to mill the apples in 1947; Aspall Hall has been in the family since 1702; Discovery apples are used in Aspall cider-making

Stopping the flood

Joan and Peter Freeman are proud of their new lake. Close to the end of their drive at Hill House Farm, it is the first and very important contributor to the Holistic Water Management Project. If the biblical rains arrive, perhaps caused by climate-change-fuelled precipitation and bursts of torrential rain, it is lakes like this that will help to slow the flow of water and protect downstream Debenham from a serious flood.

This is good news for the local community. Statistics confirm that summers and winters are getting wetter and that rainfall, when it comes, is more intense. In records going back to 1862, six of the 10 wettest years have occurred since 1998. In 1993, 33 properties in Debenham were flooded and roads rendered impassable. A number of less severe incidents have taken place since. The Freeman lake, a holding pen that can retain a mighty 6,688 cubic metres of water, is designed to deliver a more effective, natural approach to water management.

"We're looking at everything from big lakes to little ditches," says Paul Bradford, a consultant who has been working on the Holistic Water Management Project. "We can't prevent the one in 100 mega-flood, but we can take the peak off the smaller ones. All you need to do is hold the water back for 12 hours or so."

In his diary entry for 7 October 1816, Samuel Dove reminds his readers of the power of the Deben. He writes: "An extraordinary flood, considering the time of year, this day at Debenham. A Tempest early in the morning followed by intense rains, which continued with little intermission all day. The water in the river [came] within about a foot from the top of the Market Bridge…The Cherry Tree nearly covered."

Above Joan and Peter Freeman
Right The new lake at Hill House Farm

EMERIC PRESSBURGER

A
NOVELIST
SCREENWRITER
BORN MISKOLC HUNGARY
1902 – 1988

Here lies Emeric Pressburger Navigate your way over another Deben tributary to the secluded churchyard of Our Lady of Grace, Aspall, and you can pay your respects to Emeric Pressburger. Born in 1902 in Miskolc, Hungary, the celebrated international filmmaker spent the last 18 years of his life living at Shoemakers Cottage in the village. After initially working as a journalist, Pressburger began his filmmaking career as a screenwriter at UFA studios in Berlin in the late 1920s. He fled Nazi Germany in 1933, settling in London in 1935 and joining forces with the experienced director Michael Powell. The Archers, as their production company was known, made more than 20 acclaimed films, including *A Matter of Life and Death*, *The Red Shoes* and *Black Narcissus*. Pressburger died in 1988 at the age of 85.

Chapter 2
Downriver from Debenham

Imagine a waterway navigable all the way from Debenham to Woodbridge. It would connect Suffolk's agricultural heartlands with the east of the county and beyond. Barges would carry corn, cheese and other produce, and the farmers around Debenham would have a more reliable, less expensive route for their wares.

This was the proposal in 1818, when an advertisement in *The Ipswich Journal* stated: "It is intended to apply to Parliament for leave to bring in a Bill to make the river Deben navigable from the Town of Debenham to the Port of Woodbridge in this County." Dredge along the existing course of the river, ran the thinking, add the locks and other necessary infrastructure, and you would have a usable canal.

This was a time when water transport was seen as a viable alternative to the substandard Suffolk road network. "By this means," writes the landscape architect James Pulham in *Samuel Dove's Debenham*, "the Public would have the choice of Ports according to circumstances for shipping Corn…at half the expence."

What scuppered plans for a canal was the arrival of the railway, which turned water into steam and carried people and goods faster, further and for less. By 1850, England had a comprehensive rail network. Roads were also improving and the appeal of the canal began to wane.

Deben rising Towards the north of Debenham is Water Lane, which often floods in the winter to become the Deben over tarmac. The village sign honours the emergent river

Cretingham and beyond

When it leaves Debenham to the south-east, the Deben winds its way through the pretty village of Cretingham. Although unobtrusive, the river is a true presence in this part of Suffolk. It is referenced in the Cretingham sign, a striking and slightly surreal mosaic of a Viking ship under sail. The Deben also features in the work of the late artist John Western (see page 82), a regular at the Cretingham Bell who "loved the river and loved nothing more than to be sketching beside it or on it", according to his friend Gilbert Sills. And in the lounge bar at the Bell are framed photographs of a once-annual raft race on this stretch of the Deben. For many years, locals dressed up and took to the water on homemade rafts, racing between the bridges at Cretingham and Kettleburgh.

Further downstream, Brandeston Ford is an idyllic spot where cattle and other animals have been able to cross the river, a particular necessity after periods of heavy rain. Nearby, hidden in the undergrowth, is what locals claim to be a smuggler's hole, used for hiding contraband such as brandy and tobacco that was likely landed somewhere downriver, before being galloped to different parts of the county.

19

This page Ashe Abbey corn mill at Campsea Ashe **Opposite** Decoy Pond near Campsea Ashe; inside the renovated Ashe Abbey Mill; Letheringham Mill and Rackham's Mill near Wickham Market; Ashe Abbey with mill in bygone days

Loaves and fishes

In the 16th century there were more than 100 watermills in Suffolk and about a tenth of them were on the Deben. Many of the big estates had built mills to help provide food for agricultural workers. By the early 19th century the number of mills had fallen, yet they had diversified in purpose: water-powered mills were helping to make paper and oil, as well as spinning flax and grinding cement.

Ashe Abbey corn mill at Campsea Ashe, about three miles upriver from Woodbridge, operated until well after the Second World War and was originally used by a community of Augustinian nuns living at nearby Ashe Abbey. The Abbey was targeted for dissolution during the reign of Henry VIII and, as well as being linked to the changing course of religion in England, it is connected to a change in the course of the Deben. To enable them to fish more successfully, the nuns dammed the river in two places to form what is now known as Decoy Pond, a very pretty, serene spot.

Along the Deben you can see the relics of a bygone age: mills such as those at Letheringham, Glevering, Campsea Ashe and Wickham Market, which are mentioned as far back as the Domesday Book.

North-west View of Campsey-Ash.

The miller's tale

Just north of Decoy Pond, at Wickham Market, the Deben leads you to the picturesque buildings of Rackham's Mill. These days there are two reasons why you might want to visit ER & RT Rackham Ltd, and neither of them involve milling. The first is to purchase pet food, logs, solid fuel, poultry or horse feed and all the other rural products sold by the modern Rackham's. The second is the tranquillity. Here is the river at its most peaceful and calming, the perfect backdrop to the elegant mill and home to all manner of wildlife.

Swans, ducks, herons, egrets and kingfishers are a familiar sight here. The Deben, you could say, has become a sideshow at Rackham's since milling ceased in the 1970s, but it is an important one for the family and their customers. "I just love the river," says managing director David Rackham, whose family started producing flour for local bakeries in 1885 when Reuben Rackham first purchased the mill. "There's something about the water that makes this a very special place."

At the weekend, David likes nothing better than a private, drifting moment in his canoe, which he keeps close to the bank ready for an impromptu launch. "I often canoe upriver to Glevering, particularly when I'm feeling a bit fed up and in need of solace. The river here is entirely unspoiled and it's a lot cleaner than it used to be."

Rackham's has responsibilities when the waters rise and faces certain risks. "We've still got the river rights for the floodgates, so we have to control those," says David. This could mean getting up in the middle of the night when the rains are heavy and opening the sluice to create more of a flow downriver, particularly if an anxious upstream neighbour has been on the phone calling for relief. The last big flood at the premises was in 2012.

Keeping the river clear of fallen trees and other obstacles is another important responsibility, says David. "We spend a lot of money maintaining the place – clearing the weeds and cutting the trees back, which is work once done by the old National Rivers Authority." Everything needs to be managed, he suggests, even the wildlife. A cleaner river means the otters are back in numbers, which in turn has contributed to a decline in the fish population – perch, rudd and even eels, all of which were a magnet for children with their fishing rods.

Clockwise from top left Rackham's Mill was steam-driven before 1960 (note the chimney); David Rackham's grandfather, Edward, dressing a French burr millstone in 1967; the "mill men" at Rackham's in 1893 – in the centre is Reuben Rackham, founder of the mill, and the boy is Edward Rackham; machinery for grinding wheat into flour, made by Whitmore & Binyon of Wickham Market

From trickle to flow John McCarthy navigating the upper reaches of the Deben by canoe with David Truzzi-Franconi and Steve Seinet-Martin. Opposite, the canoeists can be seen stuck in fallen trees near Brandeston, emerging from a Debenham tunnel (centre) and travelling under the A12 near Wickham Market

Chapter 3
Invasion and settlement

"From the earliest times, immigrants would have come up the Deben. The Anglo-Saxons were using rivers as the trunk roads to come in and settle"

Professor Martin Carver

An elegant craft The replica half-size Anglo-Saxon longship *Sae Wylfing*

Protected by its shifting shingle bar and surrounded by a fertile valley, the Deben has been ripe for invasion throughout history. "The Deben must have been an important and useful haven from the start," says Dr Sam Newton, who runs the Wuffing Education study centre at Sutton Hoo. "Before the river walls, it would have had a vast expanse of water and been perfect for all types of maritime traffic."

The discovery of the Sutton Hoo burial ship and evidence of settlement at nearby Rendlesham indicate how important the Deben was to the Anglo-Saxons. But the recent channelling of electricity cables under the river, to connect offshore wind energy to the grid, has revealed traces of a Neolithic settlement going back thousands of years. Archaeologists found a Neolithic trackway dating from 2300BC, as well as the skull of an auroch, an extinct species of wild ox.

"From the earliest times, immigrants would have come up the Deben, which would have been an impressive, broad stretch of river," says Professor Martin Carver, who led the excavations at Sutton Hoo from 1983 to 2005. "The Anglo-Saxons were using rivers as the trunk roads to come in and settle." Sutton Hoo is believed to be the final resting place of King Raedwald, who ruled from 599-624 AD and turned the Deben estuary into a national and international centre of power. The archaeologist and historian Professor Chris Scull says that whereas Sutton Hoo was a place for the dead, Rendlesham was where this Anglo-Saxon community did its living.

"We can now be pretty certain that Rendlesham and Sutton Hoo were part of the same system of power," says Chris, who is leading a major archaeological survey at Rendlesham. "Rendlesham was their living society, the site of an East Anglian royal settlement, and Sutton Hoo was the image they wished to project in death." And Martin adds: "The River Deben is a passage of history. The Sutton Hoo-Rendlesham nexus is very much part of that story."

What remains of Walton Castle Before the Anglo-Saxons arrived in England, the Romans built a chain of forts that included Walton Castle. The castle stood defiantly on a promontory of land between the mouth of the Deben and the Orwell – land that is now largely underwater. Its remains can sometimes be seen at very low tide off the beach at Felixstowe Ferry

Mysterious mounds The Sutton Hoo site contained 18 mounds, one of which concealed Raedwald's burial ship. The boat would have been used for transport, royal visits and carrying supplies. The wide expanse of the unwalled Deben below Sutton Hoo would have been ideal waters for Anglo-Saxon ships. Ultimately, Raedwald's boat would have been dragged out of the river and up the hill for the royal burial

Mrs Pretty and Mr Brown

Basil Brown was a self-taught archaeologist, tasked by Edith Pretty in the summer of 1938 to investigate the mounds on her Sutton Hoo estate. Brown, the son of a local farmer and wheelwright, was originally employed by Pretty for just a few weeks, but after excavating two smaller mounds and finding Anglo-Saxon and Bronze Age artefacts, as well as evidence of looting, he returned to the land the following year. What he uncovered has been described as one of the most important archaeological discoveries of all time. Brown (pictured above left; above right is Edith Pretty) started work on the largest mound in May 1939, aided by the gardener John Jacobs and the gamekeeper William Spooner. After coming across neat rows of iron rivets, he then came in from the top to reveal the unspoilt shape of a 90ft (27m) longship. After some 1,300 years, what is believed to be Raedwald's last resting place had been discovered.

'The River Deben is a passage of history' Professor Martin Carver (above and far left) led further excavations at Sutton Hoo from 1983 to 2005. Professor Chris Scull (left) is now leading a major archaeological survey at Rendlesham

Valley of the kings
Aerial photographs of the Rendlesham site show the foundations of a large rectangular building, which appears as a crop mark. The consensus is that this was some kind of Great Hall, probably thatched, which housed Raedwald and his court. This community was at the very heart of Anglo-Saxon England

Where Christianity met paganism In the Venerable Bede's *Ecclesiastical History of the English People* (circa 731 AD), Rendlesham is noted as the Suffolk residence of the kings of East Anglia. It is believed that Raedwald's royal church, possibly on the site of St Gregory's (pictured, inset), had two altars, one Christian and one pagan, because Raedwald had converted to Christianity while his wife remained committed to paganism

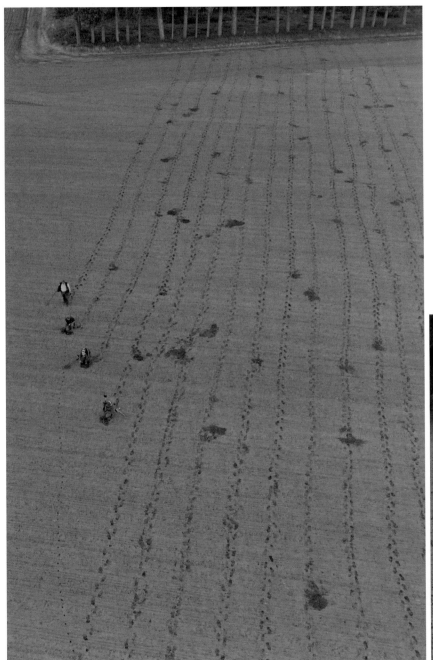

The detectorists

The discovery of a settlement at Rendlesham began with Sir Michael Bunbury. After becoming aware of illegal treasure hunting on his land at Naunton Hall, Sir Michael contacted the Suffolk Archaeological Unit. They sent in four detectorists, who have now spent more than 10 years scouring the fields for Anglo-Saxon artefacts.

Their painstaking work, which has to fit in with the farming cycle, has so far uncovered more than 5,000 items of historical interest. What the detectorists have unearthed has helped to profoundly change our understanding of Anglo-Saxon life, according to Professor Chris Scull. Indeed, the findings lead archaeologists to conclude that Raedwald was the first king of all England.

Incredible finds

"Within a few hours of being called in we were finding interesting items," says Alan Smith (pictured right), one of the detectorists. 'My personal favourite was a little gold pin with two animal heads on it. There was also an incredibly small bead, but with 64 garnets set into it.'

After three years, the detectorists realised they were dealing with an enormous settlement of about 125 acres. The navigable Deben had provided access to important maritime trade routes, and some of the coins dug up by the detectorists reveal that traders had travelled to Rendlesham from as far away as the Eastern Mediterranean.

"The detectorists have been central to the whole thing," says Chris Scull. "Without them there would be no project and we wouldn't know what we now know."

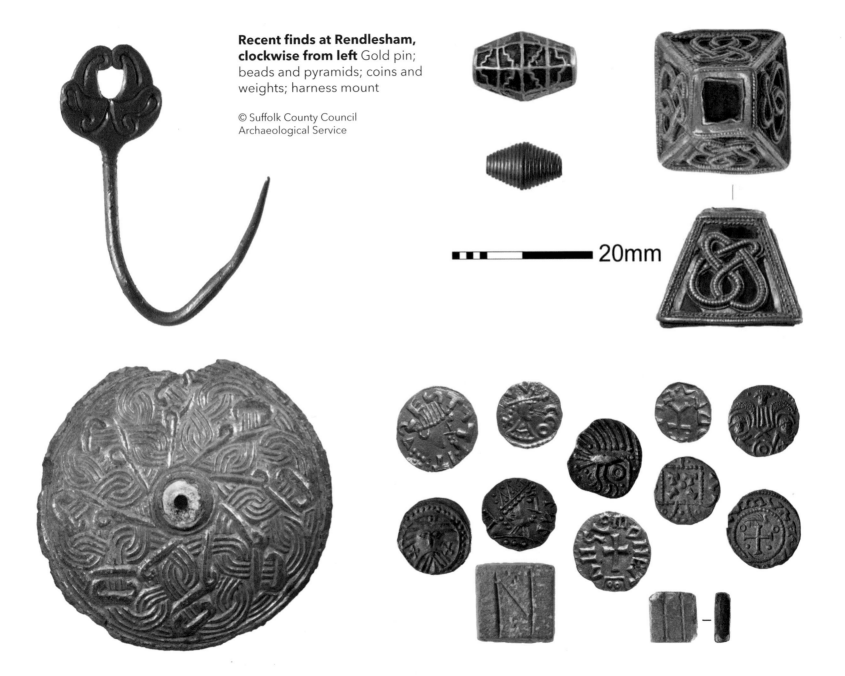

Recent finds at Rendlesham, clockwise from left Gold pin; beads and pyramids; coins and weights; harness mount

© Suffolk County Council Archaeological Service

20mm

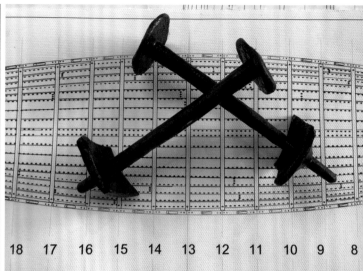

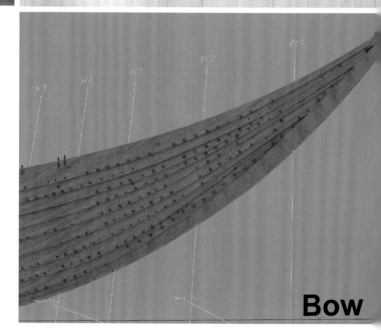

Bow

The resurrection of a ship

Plans are afoot in Woodbridge for a world first: the construction of a full-size replica of Raedwald's burial ship. The Longshed, part of the new development on the site of Whisstock's Boatyard, has been designed specifically to accommodate the build of the 90ft vessel, in an unusual private-public partnership between the developer, the Woodbridge Riverside Trust and Woodbridge Town Council.

The design of the ship is based on scientific evidence gleaned from the position of hull rivets and the impression of the hull shape left in the sand at Sutton Hoo. Southampton University and experts from around the world will engage with local shipwrights and craftsmen in a five-year programme, measuring and recording every detail of the process in order to better understand Anglo-Saxon boatbuilding techniques. Oak for the vessel is being donated from local timber sources. The ship will be taken to sea for real-life trials and the project will add greatly to international understanding of Anglo-Saxon culture and way of life.

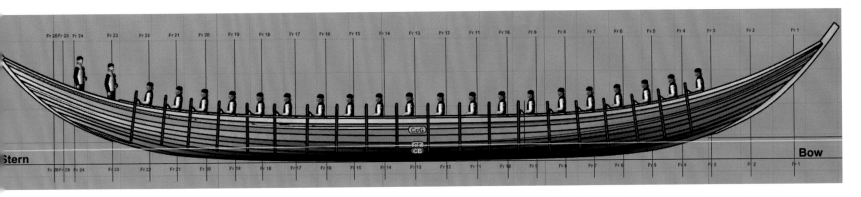

Stern

Bow

Great vessel At 90ft, the ship will dominate the Longshed. Despite its size, the original weighed only eight tonnes, owing to the amazing level of "technology" developed by the Anglo-Saxon shipwrights. Each side will be formed of only nine planks, split from green oak. The challenge will be for today's shipwrights to emulate the original techniques, using replica tools. On trials, the ship will have 40 rowers. Experiments will help us to understand whether the ship was also designed to sail, a major area of controversy among historians

Opposite An impression of the ship being built at the Longshed and rivets **This page** Computer-generated designs for the ship build

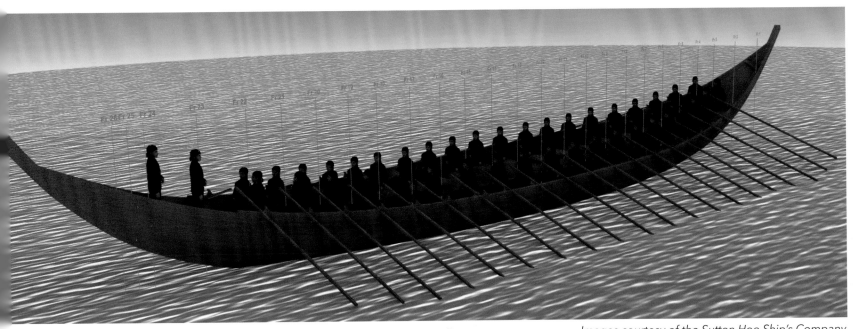

Images courtesy of the Sutton Hoo Ship's Company

SUMMER

Chapter 4
A trading river

Woodbridge on a summer's day. On the horizon you can see a ship and the North Sea

Wine, wheat, timber, coal, coprolite, cement and fish have all been part of the working life of the Deben. Pootling about in a boat today, it can be hard to imagine that this was a working river for hundreds of years. Yet trade was thriving at the mouth of the Deben long before Woodbridge (pictured) became a significant port.

The lost port of Goseford, at what is now Bawdsey, for example, was importing large quantities of wine from Bordeaux as early as the 12th century, as well as building ships for war and trading. The wealthiest merchants at that time came from places such as Bawdsey, Alderton and Falkenham, all downriver from Woodbridge. It wasn't until the 14th century that Woodbridge began to establish its dominance.

45

Woodbridge in the ascendant

As it is today, trade was tied to transport during the Middle Ages, and the downriver Deben was the most important stretch right up to the 14th century. Inevitably, this changed as new communities became established and roads were improved. For Woodbridge and its growing population, trade and shipbuilding were closely interlinked. By the 15th century, Suffolk oak was in great demand and Woodbridge merchants like John Kempe and later Thomas Marriott were making their fortunes. In his book *Suffolk Estuary: The Story of the River Deben* (1950), the historian William George Arnott writes: "The future of Woodbridge as a trading port was thus becoming more and more assured and the great ship-building era of the next century secured its development as a place of considerable importance."

The Woodbridge boom was buoyed by men like Phineas Pett, a master shipwright, who was sent to scour Suffolk for timber for the navy. Pett had a son, Peter, who married a local heiress, and in 1633 Peter Pett won the contract to build a ship for the navy at Woodbridge. The largest boat built on a slipway in the town was the 633-tonne *Kingfisher* in 1675.

'Gold rush' on the Deben

With Woodbridge established as a centre of trade and shipbuilding, other places carved out their own reputations. One such was Waldringfield, further downriver, which profited from trade in coprolite (fossilised dung) and later from its home-grown cement enterprise. Coprolite was discovered around Felixstowe in 1842 and became the catalyst for a thriving industry on both sides of the Deben. While it lasted, the coprolite boom appears to have been something of a "gold rush" on the river: more jobs, more money, more trade and a significant boost to the local economy. At the height of the industry in the 1870s, about 10,000 tonnes of coprolite a year were being shipped from the Deben and Orwell quays to Ipswich.

The Waldringfield Cement Works, which grew up in the 1890s, used a mixture of river mud and chalk. Old pictures show Waldringfield Quay littered with huge bags of chalk, brought in by barge from the Medway in Kent. The works shipped its product by sailing barge between the Deben and the Thames. At its height, the industry, which lasted until 1907, was served by 100 barges a month and accounted for a large proportion of local river traffic.

Ferry good service

Ferry House on Quayside, Woodbridge, is named for its connection to a ferry service that once ran regularly from Ferry Quay. Opposite Ferry House on the river side is the Boat Inn, now a residence, but formerly a pub dating back to the 16th century. Dropping in for a drink before or after catching your ferry would have made perfect sense.

The Deben widened downriver from Wilford Bridge and the roads were poor, so people relied on ferries at various points: Bawdsey and Felixstowe Ferry at the mouth of the river; Kirton, Ramsholt, Hemley and Falkenham further upstream. The Woodbridge ferry was revived in 1985 during the Sutton Hoo excavations and ran for five years, carrying more than 100 people on its busiest day. And as Sutton Hoo's visitor numbers grow there is the possibility of a new weekend ferry service at Woodbridge.

Age of the barges

In their heyday, barges were the vessels of trade along the Deben. They were perfect for a tidal river and performed an essential role between the 1840s and the 1930s, taking trade upriver as far as Melton. The passage of a coal barge was a real occasion and people would bring their wheelbarrows down to the quays to fill up.

The barge trade gradually declined in Woodbridge, and at the larger ports of Ipswich and Harwich, as road and rail took over. Any remaining coastal trade was managed by motor coasters. Barges can still be seen in Woodbridge, but as with the Thames barge *Melissa*, pictured on these pages, they are now used for leisure or as homes.

Birth of the boatyards

After more than 20 years of indecision, the demolition of Whisstock's Boatyard began in March 2015. The cranes moved in, the corrugated roofing came down and a new era began for the Woodbridge waterfront.

Boatbuilding has been a prosperous industry in Woodbridge over the centuries, from the largest ships of the 17th century to 20th-century classics like the Deben Four Tonner. In between were the Man-O-War naval vessels, the barges and the leisure yachts that have decorated the river since the early 20th century.

Whisstock's had been the most important yard on the Deben since it was started by Claude Whisstock in 1926. Robertson's Boatyard had been founded by Ebenezer Robertson some 50 years earlier, but Whisstock's grew to dominate the local scene. "Claude Whisstock built his business up from nothing," writes his daughter Sue in her book *A History of Whisstock's Boatyard*. "He built launches, dinghies, fishing boats, carried out repairs and then moved onto larger boats."

Whisstock's prospered in the Second World War, when the yard built an astonishing 200 boats. "They built Admiralty launches, life-boats, dinghies, fishing boats and fire float boats, all at the request of the Admiralty and often at very short notice," writes Sue.

After a spell in the merchant navy, Claude Whisstock had served his apprenticeship at Robertson's – as did Frank Knights, who also started his own yard in Woodbridge. Both Whisstock and Knights were wedded to wooden boats, even as fibreglass took over. The author and maritime historian Robert Simper says: "When the first fibreglass boat came up to Woodbridge around 1973, the story goes that Claude and Frank went to look at it after work. Both men said it was complete rubbish and would never catch on, which is why they carried on building wooden boats." Orders for wooden boats inevitably declined for all the yards.

Whisstock's thrived until the end of the 1970s, capitalising on the post-war popularity of leisure yachting. But after passing out of family ownership, the yard went into receivership in 1984, lying dormant for more than 20 years. Today, old merges with new on the Woodbridge waterfront, where what was once Whisstock's has become a mixed-use development of modern, timber-clad apartment buildings and public amenities. These include the Longshed, which was given to the town as part of the development and has become a hub for community events and traditional riverside skills. Already, young people and craftsmen have built skiffs and rowing boats, while festivals such as Maritime Woodbridge celebrate the town's history. And the Longshed is where the 90ft replica of Raedwald's burial ship will be built, right in the heart of the community.

Boats, boats, boats
Whisstock's in the yard's prime.
The four Whisstock's-built boats
lying abreast on the yard quay
were all launched in 1938

Inside Whisstock's Pictured here is the boatbuilding shed in the yard's midcentury prime, and opposite are Claude Whisstock (with pipe) and his large staff. On page 54 you can see Whisstock (still with pipe) in his office and a shipwright working on a wooden hull; he is driving screws into the hull planking with a traditional brace and bit. Boat launches were celebrated with a champagne bottle smashed across the bow and a party would be held for the new owners, friends and the yard men responsible for the build; on page 55 you can see Sue Whisstock with her father and mother at one of these parties. Launches of bigger boats were quite an event in Woodbridge.

The pride of Whisstock's The 22ft Deben Four Tonner was commissioned by Claude Whisstock in 1936 and designed by William Maxwell Blake. By 1955, 54 of these classic wooden yachts had been built and as many as 40 are still active on the east coast. Today there is a design for a new "Four and ¾ Tonner", which has more headroom and improved facilities. Four Tonners have been owned by Francis Chichester, once the world's fastest circumnavigator, who sailed one across the North Sea, and Mary Harvey Murray, who became the first woman to sail singlehanded around Britain in her Four Tonner.

Survival of the fittest

Geoff Sinton, a former director of the Woodbridge Boatyard at Everson's Wharf, says that boatyards need to be adaptable to stay afloat these days. "Today's business largely boils down to mooring, storing, hauling, shifting and lifting," he adds, as well as some maintenance work and a little bespoke building.

The Woodbridge Boatyard has operated since 1889, when Alfred Everson married the daughter of Ebenezer Robertson, who had recently taken over the Lime Kiln Shipyard – now known as Robertson's Boatyard. Sheds went up on the site of what had been a coal wharf and business flourished at Everson's new yard. Everson himself became a stalwart of the local community: a wonderful picture shows him holding a shotgun in his capacity as official timekeeper and starter for what was then the Deben Sailing Club. He kept the job for more than 40 years.

Everson's yard is steeped in history. There is a spot just off the end of the jetty that never dries out – this is where large warships are said to have been fitted out in the 16th and 17th centuries after being built upriver. The yard's somewhat rickety shed was rebuilt in 1912 after a fire that, according to the local paper, was spotted by Fred Clarke, on duty in the signal box at Woodbridge Station. The report reads: "At 3.35am he saw flames burst forth under the boat-building shop, the land there being several feet below the level of the wall and floor of the buildings. Almost immediately the buildings, which were constructed entirely of wood, seemed to be alight…The clanging of the church bell summoned the Fire Brigade, and the thrice clanging roused the whole town, and a great crowd soon lined the river wall and adjacent approaches."

Nothing was saved from the yard except a small outboard and two dinghies, according to the report. The damage and losses at Everson's, including 19 newly made boats, amounted to £1,050 – more than £100,000 in today's money – yet he was only insured for £450. This perhaps explains why his new shed was made from telegraph poles and other materials available for recycling.

That shed survives to this day and so does the yard. The current owner, Eric Reynolds, plans to create what he describes as "a centre of excellence for maritime heritage and restoration". Since acquiring the Woodbridge Boatyard in April 2019, Eric, the founder of Evolution Yachts and chair of the trustees of Save Britain's Heritage, has been repairing the shed and creating a new covered space for exhibiting and restoring traditional wooden boats. "It's so important we have a connection between the future and the past," he says.

Inside Everson's Geoff Sinton, former director of the Woodbridge Boatyard at Everson's Wharf, inside the boatbuilding shed

Chapter 5
Adapt and survive

Whisstock's Boatyard The Woodbridge yard pictured in the 1970s. Beside the shed, in line of sight with the Tide Mill, is the Wash smack *Telegraph*, which is awaiting a refit. Boatbuilding yards can seem haphazard places, but skilled hands can quickly restore wooden boats, often using timber seasoned in the open air

At home on the river Robertson's, with its live-aboard barge dock, the Tide Mill Yacht Harbour and Bass Dock beyond. Live-aboards of all kinds are a growing feature of the river, from the dockside at Granary Yacht Harbour further up, to riverside staging, to more managed facilities. Beyond that, there is a sizeable community at the head of Martlesham Creek, and more again at Felixstowe Ferry. Years ago live-aboards were mainly young people fitting out boats, but now they range from families to retirees. "For some of us it's a way of life", says Chris Landt, resident on the river in a variety of boats since 1979; for others it is simply the place they want to be, inches from water the other side of the hull, among the birds and the mudflats.

Alan Fuller talks with enthusiasm about the new-look Robertson's Boatyard. "You've got to diversify," says Alan (pictured right), who has worked at Robertson's in various capacities since 1986 and was made general manager after a change in ownership. More storage and a new workshop are part of the renaissance, he adds.

Like all the remaining boatyards on the Deben, Robertson's has had to adapt to suit changing times. Waldringfield Boatyard, for example, still offers traditional services such as mooring, lifting and storage, but it has also ventured into river trips with the launch of MV *Jahan*, a 38ft pleasure boat. Other yards are offering long-term moorings or specialist refits.

Alan is a good example of this adapt-and-survive approach. He has proved his worth to the yard through his wide experience, some of it gained nearby at Whisstock's, and his willingness to keep learning, as well as his boatbuilding education at Lowestoft College. He is currently responsible for the three main strands of the business: the movement and storage of boats; a residential mooring harbour for Dutch barges; and the workshop. New ownership at Robertson's has led to an ambitious development programme, including holiday accommodation, offices for rent, modernised workshop space and additional boat storage, which will eventually provide space for 80 or more vessels.

A less conventional sideline has been the yard's involvement in film projects such as the TV series *Shackleton*, which took Alan and colleagues to Whitby and Greenland. There was also a visit from Matt Baker and his *Countryfile* crew, who were filming an item about Arthur Ransome's boat *Nancy Blackett*.

Chapter 6
Time and tide

At the wheel Dan Tarrant-Willis, the Tide Mill's head miller and manager

A tide mill has been operating on the same riverside site in Woodbridge since 1170 and only ceased milling 800 years later. Augustinian priors owned the mill for about 350 years, until it was confiscated by Henry VIII during the Reformation. The present mill, built in 1793, is one of just two such working tide mills left in the country (the other is at Eling, near Southampton) and was opened to the public in 1973. Restoration has brought it back into use and this "living museum" once again mills flour to the rise and fall of the tide.

"The mill produces an average of 500 kilos of flour a month, rising to 700 kilos during the summer," says Dan Tarrant-Willis, head miller and manager of the Tide Mill. "In 1963 it was doing that in a day thanks to a diesel-powered hammer mill, a departure from tidal energy before the mill was restored in the 1970s." When the tide is right, visitors can see and take part in the milling process. To start the cycle, Dan may invite volunteers to turn a lever and open the sluice. This allows water from the millpond to flow in and under the mill's large wooden waterwheel, to get it turning. Only when the tide is at its lowest can the water flow from the pond under the wheel, which was installed in 2014 at a cost of £50,000.

The historic process involves a clever harnessing of natural elements. The rising tide fills a pond behind the mill via a one-way valve. Once the pond is full, no more water can get in and none can escape until it is used for milling. Milling can only take place on a falling tide so that when the sluice is opened, enough water from the pond can get under the wheel to drive it around. With the tide at its lowest ebb there is about an hour of optimum milling time, with all the power at low tide coming with the first foot of water. This is quite sufficient to keep the mill going and produce enough flour for local outlets.

Dan, a Londoner who now lives in Woodbridge, is a passionate advocate of using tidal energy in this way. "It's all about working with the environment and we are totally determined by the elements," he says. "The mill pond is a battery, saving the energy that is created by the gravitational force of the moon."

Once the waterwheel is turning, the quality of the first flour to emerge can be tested. At this stage of milling the flour is coarse, owing to the slow-turning wheel, and the grinding stones may have to be adjusted. The aim is to produce a perfectly fine flour for a select band of local bakeries and retailers, including the mill itself. Tide Mill flour is made slow and cold, says Dan. Because the milling is slow, it doesn't break up so much of the protein in the wheat, which means that bread made with Tide Mill flour should be very good for you.

The health and safety caveat is that two people need to be present at all times during milling, in case of accidents. Visitors to the Tide Mill can learn about William Bacon, who in 1870 fell into the corn hopper during his night shift. His body wasn't discovered until the morning.

Two men in a boat Simon Read and John McCarthy journeying upriver. Pictured opposite are Wilford Bridge and the old Melton Mill, where fresh water meets tidal

Force of nature

If you travel up the Deben by boat, there is a place where the river becomes non-tidal. In the *Life on the Deben* film, Simon Read, a visual artist and ecologist who for decades lived on a barge on the Deben, transports John McCarthy upriver in his diesel launch until they reach a point where they can go no further. As Simon points out, the environment changes when you reach this non-tidal part. Here the water becomes brackish, with big stretches of reed bed and perhaps a kingfisher or two.

The clearest dividing line beyond which the tide starts to peter out is Wilford Bridge at Melton, the lowest bridging point on the river. Anyone heading downriver past Wilford Bridge – in a boat or on foot – will notice the beginning of the tide for real and the start of the story of the boatyards: first Larkman's, with its haul-out and storage operation for yachts (the largest on the river), and then the more diverse Melton Boatyard, which has less space but more repair work.

A new arrival

It's amazing what the tide brings in. A surprising arrival on the river just south of the Melton Boatyard has been HMS *Vale P155*, a Swedish former fast attack craft. The 120ft (37m) vessel was towed up the Deben by two tugs on 16 July 2018, the largest ship ever to undertake such a journey. She entered the river at night, with a lengthy wait for high spring tides before heading upstream to Melton.

"The vision is several fold," says Cate Meadows (pictured above), who brought HMS *Vale* to Suffolk with Simon Skeet, the owner of Melton Boatyard. "We started by creating a Deben café and kiosk on the aft deck. Longer-term, the vision includes developing an education centre for adults and school students. The beauty of this part of the river is its nothingness. Nothing can get past Wilford Bridge except a rowing boat and we have no intention of spoiling that."

What's in a name? The 1922 motor yacht *Ginger-Dot*, moored at Melton for many years, has a fascinating history that can be told through her many identities. Built by Luders Shipyard in Connecticut, she was named *Ginger-Dot* after the daughters of the man who commissioned her, the automotive pioneer Frank Ballou Stearns. Later in the 1920s, she was bought by Colonel Charles Consolvo, who christened her *Marcon*. In 1932, *Marcon* was caught up in a tragic story when the infant son of the famous aviator Charles Lindbergh was abducted. A hoax convinced Lindbergh that the child was being held at sea and *Marcon* was used to transport him as he searched in vain for his child, who was later discovered buried in woods. Consolvo then put the boat up for sale. She turned up in England in 1940 under the guise of *Jaimie* and was requisitioned by the War Department, serving as HMS *Tormentor*. After being decommissioned she was sold for scrap, but survived and became a houseboat known as *Daystar*. In 1980, she arrived on the Deben. After 15 years at Melton, *Ginger-Dot* was brought downriver to Whisstock's by her owners, Susan and Angus Clark, as the defunct Whisstock's site was the only yard on the river large enough for her renovation. Once on site, *Ginger-Dot* became the last boat ever to be worked on at Whisstock's, as the Clarks took on four full-time employees over a seven-year period. "When we finally left the yard, they rolled up the slipway behind us," says Susan. *Ginger-Dot* then went back to Skeet's yard in Melton for another 15 years. And after 37 years on the Deben, she was towed to Fox's Marina in Ipswich (see left), where restoration work continues.

Chapter 7
Creative backdrop

Strings attached Double bassist Richard Arundel accompanying his fellow musicians onboard *Marie*

Tidal notes

River music is restless, like the tide. It ebbs and flows, lifting the spirits and soothing the soul, evoking all that is transitory and ephemeral. The tradition of music on and around the Deben is as strong today as ever. Many local musicians live and make music on boats and barges, often inspired by the river itself. "You're very much part of the elements," says Clarissa Vincent, also known as Girl in a Gale.

Clarissa creates ambient techno from her houseboat, moored in Woodbridge. Her fluid bubbles of sound can be heard on an internet radio show, Music from the River, which also features contributions from another Woodbridge musician, Jan Pulsford. She describes the Deben as a magical place that has inspired her own electronic music and live performances.

Claire Cordeaux and her partner Art Butler (pictured above left), whose band Aartwork creates music described as "psychedelic Celtic folk fusion", are refurbishing *Marie*, a 1963 Scottish fishing boat that they use as a floating stage. It was onboard *Marie* that a group of musicians performed in the *Life on the Deben* film, evoking the spirit and camaraderie of the river with their words and music.

The film featured a soundtrack of river-inspired music, including the hauntingly beautiful song *Deben Rises*, sung by Peter Hepworth (pictured above right). Andrew Osborn's gentle, unhurried classical guitar was a lilting backdrop to the scene in which John McCarthy and his fellow canoeists paddled their way through the Deben's upper reaches. Andrew, a sailor who also builds boats, hails the Deben as a peaceful, calming place that inspires his music.

The history and tradition of Deben music is closely linked to the tide. Goods such as coal and timber came up and down the river, and sailors quenched their thirst and sought entertainment in local pubs. Some played, some just listened – and then they were away with the tide. "Everything is renewed by the tide," says Jan, who co-wrote *Deben Rises* with Claire.

There is an echo of this thought in Tennyson's famous poem *Crossing the Bar*, which is said to have been inspired by a trip downriver with his friend, the Woodbridge-based writer Edward FitzGerald. The poem, which is about death, includes these immortal lines:

Sunset and evening star,
And one clear call for me!
And may there be no moaning of the bar,
When I put out to sea,

But such a tide as moving seems asleep,
Too full for sound and foam,
When that which drew from out the boundless deep
Turns again home.

Artistic landscape

Towards the end of the 1970s, it wasn't unusual to see the highly regarded Australian artist Arthur Boyd enjoying a quiet pint at the Ramsholt Arms. After a day in the studio, Boyd often strolled to the pub from his thatched cottage a few hundred yards upriver. Boyd is among a number of artists who have spent many hours working beside or close to the river, including Thomas Churchyard, George Rowe and Leonard Squirrell.

The same is true of writers. William George Arnott and Robert Simper, for example, have written extensively about the Deben. And Tennyson's friend Edward FitzGerald was living near Woodbridge when he produced the most famous English translation of a 12th-century Persian poem, *The Rubaiyat of Omar Khayyam*.

What is it about the Deben that inspires creativity? "Always there is something different," writes Arnott in *Suffolk Estuary*. "Some new viewpoint or setting of the landscape one had not noticed before, or some fresh play of light and shade to bring out the even contours of the skyline. It is a very lovely picture and I want no other for it satisfies me."

Left *Lime Kiln Quay* and **above** *Cloud Effect*, Melton, both by Thomas Churchyard (1798 -1865)

The Woodbridge Wits

Thomas Churchyard and Edward FitzGerald were part of a Woodbridge artistic and literary scene in the first half of the 19th century. Collectively known as the Wits of Woodbridge, the group also included the Quaker poet Bernard Barton and the Reverend George Crabbe, vicar of Bredfield. The group met regularly for conversation, supper, strong drink and cigars.

Churchyard and Rowe would often set up their easels to paint beside the Deben. Rowe's *Woodbridge Quay at Night* (see page 46), painted some time between 1825 and the 1840s, evokes the river and the town in all its Victorian pomp. The area has also featured in the work of John Constable. The landscape artist, known principally for his paintings of Dedham Vale on the Suffolk-Essex border, made a detailed pencil sketch of Woodbridge and the Deben in 1815, as he was travelling for a commission for Brightwell Church. "Constable was new in making the local landscape a focus of what he wanted to depict," says Emma Roodhouse, curator at the Wolsey Art Gallery at Christchurch Mansion in Ipswich, which has a fine collection of Deben-inspired art.

Churchyard, a lawyer by profession, was greatly influenced by Constable. He would steal off into the countryside, usually close to the Deben, to pursue his passion for painting. "We know that he spent each and every day painting," says the local author Robert Blake in his book *The Search for Thomas Churchyard* (1997).

Clockwise from top left Thomas Churchyard at his easel; George Rowe's (1804-1883) *Martlesham Creek at Dusk*; Churchyard the young lawyer (self portrait)

The *Scandal* of Old Fitz

Edward "Fitz" FitzGerald was an intellectual and man of letters who enjoyed sailing on his local river and beyond. This Woodbridge eccentric famously had a yacht called *Scandal* – so named, he claimed, because that was the chief product of the town. *Scandal* became a feature of the Deben, from the time Fitz launched her until long after he sold her to Sir Cuthbert Quilter of Bawdsey Manor in 1871.

Scandal was sailed around to the Deben in June 1863 after a launch at Brightlingsea. Fitz described her to a friend as "not a racer but not a Cart Horse – a Sea Boat". By August of that year, Fitz had made his first crossing to Holland. Another crossing of the North Sea followed soon afterwards and then he journeyed back to the Deben to enjoy Bawdsey Cliffs, Ramsholt and other landmarks.

FITZ GERALD'S YACHT "SCANDAL"

Clockwise from top left *Scandal* was named after Woodbridge's 'chief product'; the *Woodbridge Wits*, painted by Ellen Churchyard (1826-1909, daughter of Thomas); *The Quay at Woodbridge* by Thomas Churchyard

Lost talent

John Western (1948 - 1993) lived in Monewden and was a regular at the Cretingham Bell. With his eye for detail and his skill in the mechanics of drawing, his works have echoes of Thomas Churchyard's paintings. Western, who drowned tragically in the Deben, drew and painted prolifically, using the river as a backdrop. Today, the Deben continues to attract contemporary artists from all disciplines.

Suffolk scenes Woodbridge and Cretingham painted by John Western, pictured above

Swirls of colour

Across the Deben from where Arthur Boyd once lived and painted is the home of the contemporary artist Hugh Webster. He describes himself as a painter of tidal landscapes – swirls of colour and froth that ebb and flow against a Suffolk sky. Hugh (pictured above) lives an uncompromising, bohemian life, working from his studio in the Felixstowe Ferry Boatyard. The Deben appears to trickle into all aspects of his art. The time he spent as a studio assistant to Boyd was an important part of his development as an artist. Those parched paintings that draw on Boyd's native Shoalhaven River in New South Wales "brought more heat and variety to my work", Hugh says.

Left This old train ferry gantry, depicted by Hugh, linked the railways to Europe at Harwich, where he grew up

Clockwise from below Annie Turner in her studio, with examples of her Deben-inspired work; *River Ladders*; fossilised shark's teeth, found on the river foreshore

Water world

The Deben is at the heart of Annie Turner's work. An internationally renowned ceramicist shortlisted in 2019 for the Loewe Foundation Craft Prize, her sculptures are inspired by finds and images from the Deben foreshore. Brought up in Waldringfield, Annie sailed with her father on the river. Eroded jetties, old boats, flotsam, feathers and fossilised sharks' teeth, many collected from the Rocks opposite Waldringfield, inspire her sense of "venerable place in time and space".

Man of the river

If anyone can claim to have the Deben in his blood, it's Robert Simper. Born in 1937, the celebrated Suffolk author has written some 40 books, many of them based on his personal experience of the river. The family firm, Simpers of Ramsholt, has a diverse portfolio: food, publishing, boat charter and even riverside livery.

Born and raised in Suffolk, Robert (pictured above) briefly swapped the family farm for a spell working on the last of the Thames sailing barges. "The Deben inspires me," he says. "It's home and it changes all the time. There was a time when I knew the owner of virtually every boat on the river, but not any more."

Robert has assimilated a vast body of river knowledge, from tidal action to Viking invasion. "People often wonder why so much of the Deben remains unspoiled," he says. "This is because of the big estates, where landowners like Sir Cuthbert Quilter would not have caravan sites or chalets." Quilter was a London stockbroker who bought 3,000 acres and built almshouses, schools and sea defences, promising that nobody would go unemployed in the area.

In his books, which are well-researched and full of anecdotes, Robert outlines changes in the river and its occupation from Roman times onwards. "The Deben was a good river to use – not too difficult to get in and out and relatively easy to defend," he says. "Every time you get on the water, you see something different. It's not like going on a bus ride – there's always change and this is why the river is so fascinating."

Chapter 8
On the water

FESTIVAL TIME

Sail power

It's the Woodbridge Regatta and sails are flapping wildly at the Deben Yacht Club starting line. Boats jostle for position as they wait for the klaxon, their sails like grounded kites seeking the full force of the wind. This is an occasion that celebrates the Deben – and, today at least, sailing is the main event.

Of the three sailing clubs on the river, the Deben Yacht Club is the oldest. The 2018 Regatta marked the club's 180th anniversary and it was the same event that gave birth to the club back in 1838, Queen Victoria's coronation year. The first Regatta was held on 8 September 1838 and a notice in *The Ipswich Journal* in the days beforehand read: "A wall, adjoining the quays, a mile long, having a view of the river, extending nearly to the sea, will afford an excellent opportunity to spectators."

In those days, the river on Regatta day would have been less crowded, with fewer moorings and no formal starting lines. A shotgun would probably have started the races, as was used by Alfred Everson, the official timekeeper and starter of Deben Yacht Club races between 1889 and 1933. Eight yachts, not exceeding 10 tonnes each, were entered for a silver cup in that first Regatta, and the scene was set for a more compact and streamlined class of competitive dinghy racing. At the 2018 Regatta, many of the Toppers and Lasers and other fibreglass boats were single-handers. The two-hander dinghy classes that have been so popular on the Deben are in decline, as more and more people find single-handers are the easiest way to fit sailing into their busy lives.

Deben dinghy sailors have achieved success at the highest level. In 1936, Cyril Stollery and Dr Ken Palmer of Waldringfield trounced all comers to win the first 12ft national championship. In 1970, Peter White of Felixstowe Ferry Sailing Club won the International 505 World Championship in Hong Kong.

More recently, in 2017, Deben Yacht Club cadet Sean Woodard won the Topper 4.2 World Championships in Loctudy, France. Sean, then aged 14, was one of 215 competitors from around the world. And Ian Vidalo and Sam Carter, both of Waldringfield, have been world champions in the Lark and Cadet classes respectively.

But mainstream participation in the sport, certainly on the Deben, is going through something of a lull. "Sailing is perhaps not as cool as it used to be," says Colin Lister, commodore at the Felixstowe Ferry Sailing Club. And Malcolm Hodd, a lifelong sailor and a founder member of the Woodbridge Riverside Trust, confirms the trend: "Hectic modern lifestyles mean people set aside less time for boats. The 'weekend away sailing' is declining in popularity, even among cruisers, while increasing regulation is eroding the more Corinthian spirit of yachting." Perhaps this is the era of the solo dinghy sailor. If so, the involvement of young people through clubs such as those on the Deben will be critical to the future of the sport, Malcolm thinks.

The Royal Yachting Association has found that participation in dinghy racing has declined by more than 50% since 2002. In 2018, just three in every 1,000 people were sailing and the only growth age group for dinghy and yacht sailing has been 55-plus. Participation among 16- to 34-year-olds has fallen by 64% since 2002. But Mike Nunn, a member of Waldringfield Sailing Club for more than 50 years, feels that the club bucks the trend. "Even now there are up to 70 boats or more racing at the club every Saturday," he says. "It's very family-orientated, with a strong junior Cadet class, and you can sail at all stages of the tide."

These days, sailing is slotted in between other commitments and for that you don't necessarily need to own a boat. The Deben Yacht Club has dinghies for hire, while the Felixstowe Ferry fleet has high-performance Darts and Lasers for a breezier experience close to the river mouth and out to sea. "At Felixstowe, there's the excitement of going over the bar and this is very different from sailing in the upper river," says Colin. Past sailing enthusiasts at Felixstowe Ferry Sailing Club include the *Daily Express* cartoonist Carl Giles, who produced 30 original cartoons for the club, usually drawn for a specific social function.

Stick your oar in

Terry Davey can justifiably claim credit for a River Deben rowing boom. He was a founding member and the first captain of the Deben Rowing Club, which started at Felixstowe Ferry in the 1990s and later moved to Woodbridge. "The early club at Felixstowe took our collection of boats upstream to a Woodbridge Regatta day," Terry says. "Various Woodbridge people saw our boats and joined us for rowing at Felixstowe. As the popularity of rowing grew, the centre of activities moved more and more to Woodbridge."

Terry is a highly experienced rower, and in 2015 he sculled solo from Woodbridge to Ipswich in a boat of his own design and building. But he was not alone for the entirety of his five-hour voyage: a grey seal approached his boat in the lower reaches of the Orwell and hauled itself aboard, allowing itself to be rowed along. "It almost went to sleep at one point," Terry told the *East Anglian Daily Times*.

The number of people participating in rowing in the UK has jumped from just over 60,000 in 2010 to more than 200,000 in 2016. The sport's popularity was boosted by British successes at the 2012 Olympics and funding has followed.

A tidal river like the Deben presents a special challenge for rowers, says Jacq Barnard, current captain of the Deben Rowing Club. "You never know how wide the river is going to be or how quick the water is going to be flowing. On most rivers, when you put your boat in the water it stays where it is. Rowing on the Deben, you have to decide what you're doing straight away or you could find yourself drifting on to a mooring or another boat."

The Deben Rowing Club now has 150 members and a waiting list of would-be rowers wishing to join. But the rowing boom along this part of the Deben is not confined to the club. A donation from East Suffolk Council and the makers of the *Life on the Deben* film has allowed the Woodbridge Riverside Trust to purchase a self-build St Ayles skiff, which was constructed by a team of volunteers in the Longshed and launched in April 2019.

"Our aim is to make these projects as inclusive as possible, so that anyone with an interest in woodworking has the opportunity to take part," says the Woodbridge Riverside Trust. The St Ayles skiff, based on an original design by Iain Oughtred and named *Whisstock* in memory of the old boatyard, is an elegant 22ft, four-oar rowing boat. The trust wants it to be the first of a number of skiffs and other boats built in the Longshed – including the replica Anglo-Saxon ship.

The construction of the skiff, the first boat to be built and launched from the Whisstock's site for 30 years, helped inspire Jacq to found the Woodbridge Coastal Rowing Club. Some of the skiff builders have now joined the club and so continue to enjoy the boat, this time on the water. The two rowing clubs, and the community-led building programme in the Longshed, mean rowers will continue to make a splash on the Deben.

This page The first St Ayles skiff under construction in the Longshed
Opposite Rowers on the river and Jacq Barnard, captain of the Deben Rowing Club

AUTUMN

Chapter 9
Halfway down

Ship shape The Waldringfield Boatyard, founded in 1921. Today, the yard is run by Mark Barton

Waldringfield has played a key part in much of the Deben's history. In earlier times, the village enjoyed uninterrupted views down to the mouth of the river and up to St Mary's Church in Woodbridge. Now trees have grown up, but it is still possible to spot the lookout hut in front of Waldringfield's public car park. From here, river pilots could see vessels coming into the Deben entrance and they would row down on the tide to pilot ships up the river on the flood. The hut was used as an observation post during both wars.

In the 19th century, Waldringfield was a centre for coprolite-digging. Later, when cement became the major industry in the area, the village housed the cement works. Chalk was imported from Kent and mixed with sediment from the Deben, before being fired in kilns alongside the river. So significant was the site that it had its own light railway to transport material from the beach to the kilns.

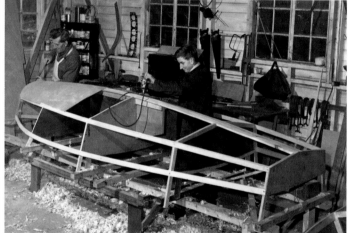

Clockwise from above Harry Nunn (left) started Nunn's yard in 1921 with his friend and colleague Corky Edmunds; Peter White, who later became 505 World Champion building an OK Dinghy; the Dragonfly fleet jockey for position at Waldringfield; George Turner with his suitably attired daughter Peggy – George hired out dinghies from the beach

The beach huts along the foreshore, erected on flat areas created by coprolite-digging under the cliff, reflected the changing times. The first wartime "round hut" for housing troops was built in 1919 and still stands, while a second hut became the headquarters for the sailing club as the sport grew in popularity. In the Second World War, Waldringfield was closed for Operation Quicksilver, with restricted access even for residents. The operation involved the building of fake landing craft and dummy army encampments, designed to fool enemy reconnaissance aircraft.

In recent years, threats to Waldringfield come more from the sea. Early in 2013, work began on a vulnerability study. The tidal surge in December that year, which led to the flooding of many riverside properties, provided the spur to raise funds locally, match-funded by the Coastal Communities Fund. Spoil was dug out from behind the sea wall, creating the Dairy Farm Marsh Nature Reserve on land owned by the Waller family, and the Internal Drainage Board provided the design for the defences and saltmarsh protection. Wildlife conservation was key to the plan.

Boats have played an increasing role in the life of the village. Mike Nunn tells how his father, Harry, started the Waldringfield Boatyard in 1921. Harry, who had a workshop near the river, decided to rent half of the old cement works quay to expand his business. Local boys helped to move the workshop across the road to the quay, borrowing every old wheel they could find. Harry ran the yard with his younger brother, Ernie, for many years.

Boats such as the Dragonfly dinghy and the larger Dragon helped to make the Waldringfield Boatyard's reputation for wooden boats. "Nunn's and the Robertson's yard upriver built about 45 Dragonflies between them," says Mike. Dragonflies are still a class boat and in 2019 their 70th anniversary was celebrated with a regatta at Waldringfield that attracted 15 Dragonflies, three from Ireland.

Above The Waldringfield Cement Works; Harry Nunn carrying out repairs at the yard

Free spirits John Archer, pictured here with his partner Lizzie and their son, is carrying on the Deben tradition of independent-minded sailors. In the 1970s and 80s, there was a moving population of people who converted boats not as houseboats, but to take off on voyages across the oceans. Work was merely a means of making money to help prepare your boat for sea. John, who appeared in the *Life on the Deben* film, bought his boat, a dilapidated former fishing craft, for £1, patched it up and sailed it from Kent to Waldringfield. The hull is now sound and the family plan to live aboard when the boat is ready.

101

Chapter 10
The disappearing village

Sacred place Ramsholt Church has a distinctive round tower

Clockwise from this image The slip at Ramsholt beside the quay; a bird's-eye view of All Saints Church; Church Cottages before they were demolished (in 1962) and seen in a painting; Elm Row, unoccupied since the 1980s; John McCarthy enjoys the view towards Kirton Creek from the church tower

Downriver from Waldringfield is the village of Ramsholt, which perhaps illustrates best more recent change on the Deben. In the 1880s, the parish was a lively community of more than 130 residents. A ferry (started in 1502) ran regularly across the river to Guston in Kirton Creek. The Deben was a primarily a means of transport. Ramsholt Quay was visited by barges serving nearby farms until the 1930s, but not many people ventured as far as Ipswich even then. This was a quiet rural community focused on farming. But as farm practice changed, so did the demand for labour, and by the 1970s most of the cottages had been demolished, with residents rehoused to local villages.

Today, the Ramsholt Arms is the first port of call for boats visiting the river. Many are welcomed by the harbour master, George Collins, who took over from his father, "Old George", in 1984. George looks after some 200 boats on the moorings either side of the fairway. Access to the hard is now secured for the community after a long legal battle led by George and the Fairways Committee at the turn of the millennium.

The walk from the quay to Ramsholt Church is as fine as any in Suffolk, either across Dock Marsh when the weather serves, or on footpaths past the old schoolhouse in The Street, the centre of the village. The school closed in 1927 and it is said that the 50 or so pupils were issued with bicycles (known as "educational bicycles"), torches and capes for the journey to their new school in Alderton.

Like so much early history, solid facts about Ramsholt are hard to come by. Was the church's rare round tower really a lookout for Anglo-Saxons watching for invading Danes, or did it date from early Norman times? Certainly, the view from the tower stretches right down the river and there may well have been an Anglo-Saxon observation post there. But the church's nave, chancel and doorways are now dated c. 1300. A painting from 1790 shows Ramsholt Church in "great disrepair" – it was restored at the beginning of the 20th century by the Quilter estate.

But never mind the dates. Ramsholt's atmosphere, serenity and sense of history – possibly 1,000 years of time and people passing – lingers in the mind long after a visit. Perhaps here beats the very heart of the Deben.

Risky business A smugglers' passage beneath Alderton Church leading to the manor house was revealed to John McCarthy by church warden Barry Vincent (pictured right)

Smugglers' tales

Smuggling has thrived on the Deben for centuries. These days, drugs and sometimes people are landed at the mouth of the river, but in the 18th century, spirits, tobacco and other contraband were quietly rowed ashore at places like Bawdsey, Ramsholt, Martlesham Creek and Woodbridge before being distributed to other parts of the county.

By its nature, smuggling is a secret business, so smugglers' tales are frequently just that. But in the *Life on the Deben* film, Barry Vincent, warden of Alderton Church, shows John McCarthy a secret smugglers' passage under the church. The tunnel links to the Swan pub and the manor house (pictured far right). It is certain that there were lights and signs to warn smugglers of the presence of revenue men.

Inevitably, there are Deben smuggling stories aplenty, like the one where smugglers threw their cannons overboard on the river near Woodbridge to allow a swifter escape from the pursuing customs cutter. Or the tale of Margaret Catchpole, reputedly born in 1762 in nearby Nacton, who fell in love with "local" smuggler William Laud and was eventually deported to make a new and very successful life for herself in Australia.

Chapter 11
Saltmarsh and siltation

Man of the marshes Simon Read repairing a brushwood fence of his own construction

In a scene from the *Life on the Deben* film, Simon Read is repairing a brushwood fence in a saltmarsh. Clad in full-length waders and carrying a hefty bundle of wood, he is squelching through the mud, looking at every step as if he could be sucked under. This is estuary management in the raw and Simon has been at the frontline for more than 20 years.

His first impression of the Deben when he arrived in Woodbridge almost four decades ago was of a very crowded river. "As you get to know a place, it gets under your skin," says the artist and ecologist. "The more familiar I became with the river, the more my interest grew in its systems and the way that they work." His art, he suggests, goes hand in hand with his commitment to the river and its wellbeing.

In 2008, Simon was one of the founder members of the Deben Estuary Partnership (DEP), set up to consider issues such as flood protection, how to preserve the tranquillity of the river and how best to manage those vulnerable saltmarshes. The Deben Estuary Plan, compiled by the DEP, is the management plan for the estuary, signed off by the Environment Agency and the local authority. It is revised every five years and provides guidance to all those involved with the river.

"Saltmarshes are a dynamic system," says Simon. "If sediment is lost from one part by erosion, it may accumulate somewhere else. The key aim of the partnership is to foster an appreciation of the estuary as an integrated organic system, and through this encourage the community to become actively engaged in the management process."

The River Deben Association, set up in 1992 and a partner in the DEP, has more than 900 members. It has a saltmarsh research group to monitor what is happening. "There is significant erosion but also some accretion, and work to use dredgings for restoration purposes seems to be going well," says the association's chair, Sarah Zins.

Simon has produced a large-scale map of the estuary (see overleaf) to identify those areas most vulnerable to flooding. The issue of tidal erosion raises questions about the need to protect land, including productive agricultural land alongside the Deben. What are the trade-offs, for example, between tranquillity and access, land use and flood protection, agriculture and the environment? Another question is how to pay for flood protection. One option identifies "enabling development", where the landowner agrees to sell land for development to fund flood management.

Simon's work with saltmarshes involves placing a porous brushwood fence in the path of the tide, making it possible to slow the flow on the flood and hold it back on the ebb so that sediment is retained and hopefully the potential for loss of material reduced. This allows beleaguered saltmarsh sites to recover, providing nutrient-rich food and shelter for young fish, and acting as a localised carbon sink.

"We are experiencing incremental sea-level rise and the saltmarshes are beginning to show signs of stress," says Simon. "Consequently, it is vital that any strategies for saltmarsh protection are developed in the context of estuary systems."

The Deben floodplain: an original work by Simon Read

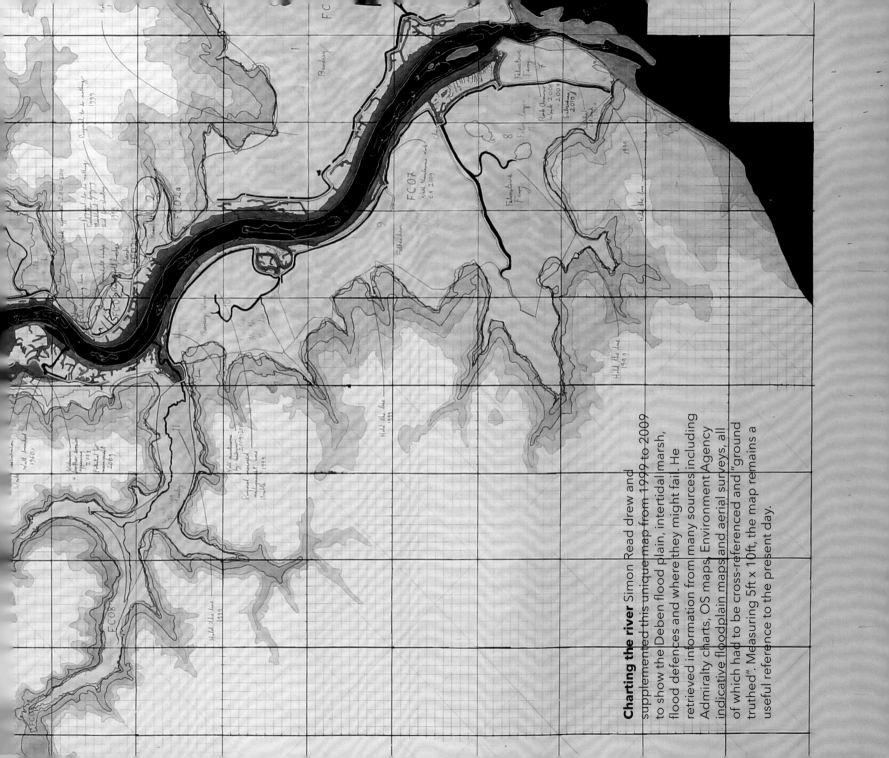

Charting the river Simon Read drew and supplemented this unique map from 1999 to 2009 to show the Deben flood plain, intertidal marsh, flood defences and where they might fail. He retrieved information from many sources including Admiralty charts, OS maps, Environment Agency indicative floodplain maps and aerial surveys, all of which had to be cross-referenced and "ground truthed". Measuring 5ft x 10ft, the map remains a useful reference to the present day.

Engineering with mud

Tam Grundy is operating a hydraulic grab on a barge docked at Woodbridge. This is the engineering end of saltmarsh restoration and Grundy is the specialist on the Deben. "The river has been silting up for years," he says. "We take the mud from where it's not wanted and put it where it's needed."

Growing up downriver in Bawdsey, Tam enjoyed a childhood beside the river and on boats. A well-respected local tugmaster, he now owns a couple of small tugs, a lighter barge and a dredger, which he operates out of Melton Boatyard. He is responsible for mooring maintenance on much of the upper Deben estuary and is on hand to solve any problem to do with moving boats, no matter how large. Much of his work is on the Orwell, in Harwich, and further upriver.

Dredging and reusing the silts to restore saltmarsh is an extension of his river work. "Every river suffers from siltation and the Deben has real problems," Tam says. "Removing the mud brought up by dredging provides an instant, proper fix."

Dredge and deposit Tam Grundy's dredger. He says the Deben has 'real problems' with siltation

Tam works as an independent operator for private clients on the Deben. He recently removed 700 tonnes of sediment from Bass Dock, opposite Woodbridge railway station on the waterfront, to Loder's Cut island, off Kyson Point.

All his dredging and disposal work is subject to prior approval from the government's relatively new regulatory body, the Marine Management Organisation, which requires a licence (and a fee) to undertake these activities. Working through the licensing process, Tam and his colleague Carol Reid have demonstrated a practicable solution to the dredging needs of the river. "It's a win-win situation," he says. "As at Kyson, you recover depth in one part of the river and height in another."

And depth clearly matters in the upper reaches of the Deben. "The channel is generally clear, but the sides are constantly filling in," says Simon Skeet, the owner of Melton Boatyard. "Every other year, we have to take all our berths out and we dredge them. If I could dig out another 100 berths, I could sell them in under a month." And Tam would be the man to do it.

Chapter 12
Wild side

Over the summer months, the "klep, klep" of oystercatchers is a familiar sound along the tidal part of the Deben. Upriver in narrower, woodier sections, you might spot the flash of a kingfisher or the wings of a soaring barn owl. Make your way through some of the more overgrown parts of the riverbank and you could catch sight of an otter.

Thanks to the mud and tidal sustenance, the Deben estuary has been designated a Site of Special Scientific Interest for certain species of wading birds and wildfowl, and for the saltmarsh that acts both as a habitat and a barrier against the tide. Migrants on and around the estuary include the avocet, once virtually extinct in the area, the black-tailed godwit, the curlew, the grey plover and the redshank. This is also a Special Protection Area for wintering avocet and brent geese, and an internationally important Ramsar site for its role as a wetland and, importantly, a haven for wintering birds.

"The state of wildlife on and around the river reflects the fact that it is in pretty good health," says Penny Hemphill from the Suffolk Wildlife Trust. "There have been changes in land use, but it's still a fantastic habitat for all types of species."

Waders at large A curlew (above) and an oystercatcher with chick (left) **'A fantastic habitat'** Penny Hemphill (opposite) of the Suffolk Wildlife Trust

Making connections

Penny should know, having explored the length of the Deben as part of a survey for the Environment Agency. The aim of the survey was to find out where the health of the river could be enhanced – for example, by varying its flow through restoration projects, working wherever possible in partnership with landowners and farmers.

"The entire catchment is important, from its headwaters through the middle reaches to the estuary. Issues such as sedimentation and run-off from arable land, together with abstraction pressures, occur throughout," Penny says. Trees have a vital role to play (see overleaf), she adds, not just because of the benefits they bring to the river itself, but as part of the wider movement to rebalance the climate and restore wildlife habitat. Like many rivers in East Anglia, the historic use of the Deben has left a legacy of varying structures that can form a barrier to the movement of species along the river.

Another important part of Penny's work, with the Suffolk Wildlife Trust and other organisations such as the Deben Estuary Partnership, is to work with local farmers and landowners, who themselves make an important contribution to conservation.

The otters are back

One conservation success story has been the return of otters to the banks of the Deben, and to other rivers throughout the UK. Otter numbers plummeted in the mid-20th century because of hunting and particularly river pollution, but cleaner waters, improved habitat and a hunting ban in 1978 have brought this mammal back with a vengeance. Top of the riverine food chain, otters indicate a healthy, diverse aquatic environment and they are now widespread throughout Suffolk's rivers.

Another success has been the return of the water vole, which would have undoubtedly become extinct by now without special measures. This indigenous animal is still in decline in much of the UK, but not any longer in East Anglia. A sustained conservation project has involved working with landowners to restore wetland habitat in conjunction with controlling American mink. Mink is an example of a non-native species that can wreak havoc upon local wildlife, particularly the water vole. The animal is small enough to invade water vole burrow systems and can wipe out a whole population in a matter of days.

The Deben Estuary Plan notes the importance of protecting wildlife habitats along the lower reaches of the river, highlighting dykes, reed beds, grazing marsh and even arable land as habitats that can help to maintain the diversity of species that gives the area its character. Penny Hemphill explains that flows in the Deben's upper catchment are heavily influenced by rainfall, meaning that the smaller tributaries can dry out in the summer months. This, together with abstraction, has a knock-on effect on flows lower down the catchment. "Nature adapts to climatic conditions, but we can help it to be more resilient by working with landowners to enhance the riverine habitat," Penny says. "The Deben has perhaps the most beautiful and timeless estuary in the eastern region, and successful partnerships with all those involved with the river will be key to its future health."

Digging deep Trees being planted at Home Farm in Kettleburgh

Root and branch

More than 50 riparian trees have been planted on the banks of the Deben, at Home Farm near Kettleburgh.

The new trees and shrubs – a selection of local species including alder, black poplar, goat willow, buckthorn, blackthorn and dogwood – should support a wide range of animals and plants. The root systems will help to stabilise the river banks, provide habitat for fish and reduce sedimentation, while shading from the trees will help to control water temperatures and excessive aquatic plant growth, as well as providing enhanced habitats for other species.

The trees, planted by the Suffolk Wildlife Trust in partnership with the Environment Agency, have been funded by profits from the *Life on the Deben* film.

"This project, initiated by the Suffolk Wildlife Trust, is an excellent example of working together in partnership to improve the River Deben," says Naomi Boyle of the Environment Agency.

Chapter 13
The lost port

Hidden history Is this all that remains of Goseford?

Searching for Goseford Peter Wain shows John McCarthy where he believes the heart of the port was located

At the mouth of the Deben, Bawdsey was once a thriving centre of trade, shipbuilding and wealth, as was neighbouring Alderton and a number of villages on the Felixstowe side of the river. All of them were grouped around the lost port of Goseford. The forensic investigations of the historian Peter Wain are helping to further our understanding of this once-great port. "I'm like a pig rooting for truffles," says Peter, somewhat disarmingly. "It would be very interesting to dig down here and see what is there."

For a period of about 150 years, between 1250 and 1400, Goseford was one of England's key ports. The size and number of ships, taxes paid, services to the Crown and the wealth of the local population all point to the fact that Goseford once ranked alongside London, Dartford, Bristol, Great Yarmouth and other major English ports in the supply of ships for trade and war.

In his paper *The Medieval Port of Goseford*, Peter provides a catalogue of evidence for the existence of this thriving port and the affluence of the local population. The heart of the port, he believes, was somewhere between Alderton and Bawdsey. The two villages grew rapidly in the 13th century and, according to Peter, the villages on both sides of the Deben had a collective population of about 1,500 – the size of a small medieval town.

William George Arnott A Woodbridge-based estate agent and historian, WG Arnott was a lifelong sailor who wrote several landmark books about Suffolk rivers, including *Suffolk Estuary: The Story of the River Deben* (1950). His books are heavily researched yet full of fascinating stories; the historian Robert Simper describes them as "pioneering works on Suffolk's maritime history". Arnott (pictured right) was a libertarian and, according to Simper, believed strongly that the Deben should be an open river on which everyone should do as they pleased. He opposed the establishment of mooring committees and was appalled by the use of concrete on river wall defences. No doubt he would have been dismayed by today's rules and regulations.

WG Arnott, in his book *Suffolk Estuary*, notes that the area just inside the mouth of the river was first defended by the Romans and then colonised by the Anglo-Saxons, who saw it as an ideal haven for ships and trade. Goseford thrived because of its proximity to the sea. Communications by land were poor and rivers like the Deben were the trunk roads of their age.

Peter cites the evidence of a map drawn in 1250 by the Benedictine monk Matthew Paris, which includes Goseford as a centre of maritime activity – one that was asked by the Crown to build ships for naval purposes. In 1338, no fewer than 15 Goseford ships set sail from the Deben as part of Edward III's expedition to Flanders.

"It's a matter of great regret that we don't have records from the port itself, but we know the names of many of the skippers and boats that came from Goseford," says Peter. "Villages on both sides of the river were working together. They were required by the King to build ships and they couldn't have done it without collaborating."

Ancient evidence Peter Wain and John McCarthy consider a 13th-century map referencing Goseford

Goseford ebbs away

At Goseford's peak as a shipbuilding centre, the locals also built their own (sub-200 tonne) boats on the Deben. This would have involved simply digging out a scoop behind a barrier with the river, and knocking away the barrier when the boat was ready to go – a bit like a medieval version of a modern dry dock.

Goseford's significance began to wane at the beginning of the 15th century. The effects of the Black Death, piracy, general economic uncertainty and inundations by the sea all contributed to the port's decline. Other reasons included the advent of bigger ships and new methods of shipbuilding, which aided the rise of Woodbridge as the Deben's most important port.

England was still at war with France, and vessel after Goseford vessel was seized as trade between the two countries virtually ceased. The port gradually disappeared from the radar – more than 500 years before radar itself was to haul Bawdsey back into the spotlight.

Queensfleet This was believed to be a major artery between the Deben and the North Sea, with Goseford at its heart

Chapter 14
We know you're coming

Rural sprawl Bawdsey Manor is an architectural oddity

RADAR BULLETIN

Victory Souvenir Number ~ 1945

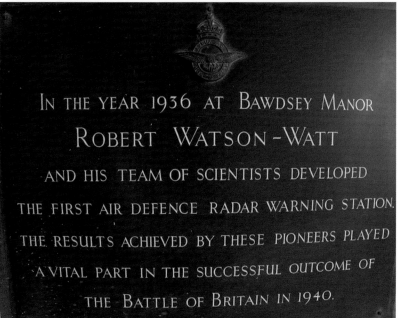

IN THE YEAR 1936 AT BAWDSEY MANOR

ROBERT WATSON-WATT

AND HIS TEAM OF SCIENTISTS DEVELOPED

THE FIRST AIR DEFENCE RADAR WARNING STATION.

THE RESULTS ACHIEVED BY THESE PIONEERS PLAYED

A VITAL PART IN THE SUCCESSFUL OUTCOME OF

THE BATTLE OF BRITAIN IN 1940.

The coming of radar

Bawdsey Manor dominates the mouth of the Deben, its gables and towers acting as a powerful statement of English eccentricity. The building is a wonderfully bizarre clash of architectural styles. A tribute to late Victoriana and the Empire, Bawdsey Manor, perhaps appropriately, also became the world's first operational radar station.

The manor is the creation of its original owner, Sir Cuthbert Quilter, who acquired the title of Lord of the Manor of Bawdsey in 1883. The businessman and stockbroker, and MP for Sudbury from 1885 to 1906, spent 18 years extending the manor when he decided to make it his main residence.

His building remained part of the Quilter estate until 1936, when the radar pioneers Robert Watson-Watt and Arnold Wilkins came in search of a new base for their highly secretive work. The manor was purchased for the sum of £24,000 and the Bawdsey Research Station was born.

"My mum worked at the manor, where she met my father," says the Bawdsey resident Mary Wain. "They were both in the RAF and joined up before the war and came to Bawdsey." By that time the building was full of scientists, as the country sought to bolster its defences in the face of Nazi aggression.

On 24 September 1937, Bawdsey became the world's first fully operational radar station and went on to provide a vital early-warning system during the Battle of Britain in 1940. Mary and others believe that not only did radar (an acronym for radio detection and ranging) help the RAF to win the battle, but it also helped to delay and ultimately end any prospect of a German invasion.

By the end of the Second World War, up to 80% of leading British physicists were involved in the development of radar, which today is at the heart of everything from air-traffic control to weather forecasting and machine learning.

Opposite WAAFs at work (top right); sailboats and view across to the transmitter towers (bottom right) **Above left** Local resident Mary Wain, whose parents both worked at Bawdsey Research Station

This image Mary Wain and John McCarthy at the Bawdsey Radar museum
Below The room Winston Churchill stayed in at the Bawdsey Research Station

Scientists on the frontline

Mary Wain's connection with the past lives on: she is an enthusiastic trustee of Bawdsey Radar, a museum now located in the original transmitter block. This bunker-like concrete building, restored with the help of a Heritage Lottery Fund grant, tells the story of radar via an evocative audio-visual display.

If you want to get a feel for early detection systems, this is the place to come. The displays may be modern but the building itself remains completely authentic – one of the conditions of the grant. They must have been lonely times for the folk who operated the four transmitter towers from this command-and-control bunker.

Working inside the manor itself would have been more convivial, with its mix of scientists and military personnel, including the radar operators. But nobody knows exactly how many people worked there, Mary says, because the work was so confidential.

It is perhaps no surprise, given the importance of the Bawdsey Research Station, that Winston Churchill himself paid a visit to the manor and slept in one of the bedrooms.

Bawdsey Ferry

The Deben helped to keep the Bawdsey Research Station's personnel connected with the outside world. On the other side of the river was the tempting prospect of a night out, or at least a drink. Felixstowe Ferry, a three or four-minute boat ride away, was closer than the pub in Bawdsey and, as Mary says, being on the water can be a liberating experience, even for a few minutes.

The history of the ferry between Bawdsey and Felixstowe goes back to Norman times and it remains an important link between the two communities and their visitors today. The local Brinkley family has close associations with the service: Charlie Brinkley obtained a licence to operate the ferry in 1931, followed by his son Charlie Junior and his grandson Robert. Between them, the Brinkleys served as ferrymen for more than 100 years, and when Robert swapped ferrying for fishing in 1999 it was the end of an era. Today, the Felixstowe Ferry Boatyard runs the service.

Above left and right Bawdsey Research Station personnel using the ferry service
Left Charlie Brinkley Senior began running the ferry service in 1931

WINTER

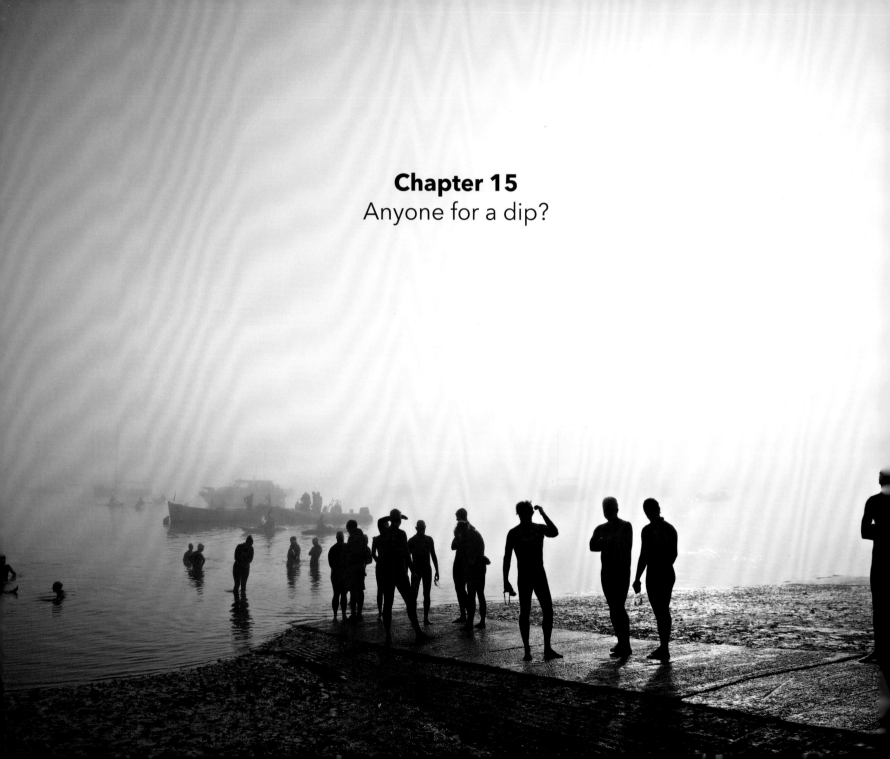

Chapter 15

Anyone for a dip?

Plunge into the Deben during the summer months and you can expect water temperatures of up to 18C - cooler than a heated swimming pool, yet invigorating when the heat of the day starts to wear you down. But in January or February, when the east wind really bites, river temperatures can fall below 3C.

Simon Rudland (pictured above, wearing head-cam) is one of a group of hardy swimmers who brave the Deben throughout the year. Swimming in freezing February, he says, is all part of the experience. To swim in the river is to commune with nature and it delivers a high that, for some, is as much a therapy for the mind as it is for the body. "It's that Ganges thing," says Simon, a GP who swims at Waldringfield three or four times a week. "You leave the water feeling completely refreshed - it's an immersive experience, a going back to the womb, which perhaps we all gravitate towards."

But Simon is mindful of the tides, the cold, the boats and the other risks that come with swimming in a natural body of water. "You are in an environment that can be either a friend or a foe," he says. The most important thing, he adds, is to arm yourself with knowledge about where you are swimming and to make sure someone else is around in case you get into difficulty. Information on the dangers of open-water swimming is available from the Royal Society for the Prevention of Accidents.

Water therapy

Deben swimmers cover the whole spectrum of ability, including some serious athletes. The tidal waters of the lower reaches offer swimmers a constantly changing environment in terms of the movement, flow and feel of the water. Swim against the flood of a rising tide and you can find yourself engulfed by cold seawater. Swim back on an ebb tide and you may be surrounded by pockets of upriver warmth.

The Deben has its clubs, but swimming is not yet among them. For the most part, swimmers meet informally at Felixstowe and Waldringfield and choose their route accordingly. Events are starting to arrive: a 10K swim from Bawdsey to Waldringfield, for example, and the prospect one day of a Deben triathlon.

Wild swimming is a zen sport, according to Simon Rudland, which is why it can be so good for mental as well as physical health. "Perhaps you're bringing your demons to the river and dealing with them, but it's an experience you are having with other people. There's a collective sense of clearance that leaves us all feeling different," he says. Plus, you never quite know what to expect. When Simon and two friends swam from Bawdsey to Woodbridge, they had a surprise companion – a friendly seal.

Taking the plunge A midwinter swim from Felixstowe Ferry to Bawdsey and back again. Not for the faint-hearted!

Chapter 16
The harbour master

Where river meets sea
Felixstowe Ferry and the shingle
bar at the mouth of the Deben

John White has been the Felixstowe Ferry harbour master for some 20 years, following 42 years as a shipwright in the local boatyard. His father was a fisherman but John wanted to learn a trade; he started work in the boatyard at 16 and helped to build fishing boats as well as yachts and dinghies.

In his present role he is responsible for the safe passage of boats in and out of the Deben. He must also manage the 240 moorings along this stretch of the river: leisure yachts and working fishing boats, most of which were built in the boatyard.

The harbour master is always on call, dealing with everything from enquiries about moorings for the night to advising yachtsmen on tides and how to safely negotiate the shingle bar. John has his own website, debenestuarypilot.com, which offers a useful guidance map of the river entrance, as well as information on prevailing winds, weather and other local intelligence.

John must also keep an eye out for illicit cargo: drugs, goods and even people. He has plenty of stories about inflatables abandoned on the beach after probable drug runs and even a mini-submarine that it is believed could have been bringing in arms for the IRA.

People trafficking is a concern along this remote part of the coastline. In 2016, a group of people were seen being taken off a yacht at Bawdsey Quay and then loaded into a Range Rover; later that day, six people jumped out of a Range Rover at a pub in Bromeswell and fled into the woods. In 2014, three people were jailed for participating in an illegal operation bringing immigrants into the UK at Orford Quay.

The harbour master is at the frontline of defence against smuggling and trafficking, as he has been throughout history.

Opposite Felixstowe Ferry harbour master John White
This page Lobster fishermen; crabbing
on the quayside

Chapter 17
Protecting the future

Sea view Felixstowe Ferry at the entrance to the Deben

For Maritime Woodbridge, the riverside is alive with people. The Tide Mill, the Longshed, the Cruising Club and the Deben Yacht Club are all crowded with visitors. There are barges decked out with nautical bunting, a Viking re-enactment and live music paying homage to the sea shanties of old. In this kind of atmosphere there is a sense that the heart of Woodbridge, the very spirit of the town, is shifting back down to the river. Woodbridge Waterfront, the new development on the site of Whisstock's Boatyard, is putting on a show for this summer event and the public is responding with enthusiasm.

Tourism and visitor attractions are one aspect of today's life on the Deben. Visitors flock to Sutton Hoo, soaking up the history and viewing the river in all its glory, but how do you reconcile tourism with the needs of the Deben and its natural environment? The Deben Estuary Plan is the official management strategy for the estuary and is renewed every five years. Published in 2015 and now under review, it highlights the need for "responsible access" to the tidal river – the stretch where walks, boating and other pastimes take centre stage.

This image The river wall along the Deben **Opposite** The Woodbridge riverside

Strolling along the smart new waterfront, it's hard not to wonder about future development along the Deben. There is a fine balance to be struck between giving people a natural riverside experience and offering somewhere for them to park the car and have a drink or a cup of tea. And what about providing them with somewhere to live? The Local Plan, which provides government guidance for future strategies, lists residential schemes now being built and all proposed plans, including possible garden cities such as the one suggested for the Felixstowe area. If all this new building goes ahead, a further 8,000 homes will be constructed around the Deben Estuary.

The tidal surge of December 2013 was a wake-up call for the estuary. Flood protection work in Woodbridge and downriver has increased and the Waterfront development sits behind robust concrete and glass barriers. It's a response that has stretched the resources of all those involved, notably the Environment Agency and local landowners.

Having a say

Landowners, farmers and local residents are all being encouraged to have their say about issues affecting the Deben. The artist and ecologist Simon Read (see page 110) stresses the importance of talking to people about what they want for their river. "It's about asking the question as to whether something is manageable or not," he says. How much flood protection and who pays? What is the scope for landowners to fund flood defence work by selling off land for development? Which bits of the riverside need intervention and which can be left alone?

According to Karen Thomas, who heads up East Suffolk Council's Coastal Partnership East, the key challenge is to come up with clever, thrifty solutions that work for all parties. For example, a combination of improved flood defences and more sensible water management, which are arguably two sides of the same coin. In the aftermath of the 2013 tidal surge, landowners and farmers had a renewed focus on the importance of protecting their land from flooding and the salination of irrigation water, while placing emphasis on the need for better access to affordable freshwater supplies for crop irrigation.

"Flood protection along the Deben valley is very important for our vegetable production," says the farmer James Foskett. "The tidal surge knocked out 60 metres of our newly rebuilt 1,200-metre wall. This section was 'protected' by the Environment Agency [EA] because of the presence of a whorl snail colony. Saltwater coming into the breach for the following six months killed everything from grass to trees and newts to water voles in 80 acres of our land."

While the EA provided initial funds for the wall, it was up to the landowner to repair and then maintain it, he explains, with the repair costing more than the original EA wall funding.

All ended well, however. "The land value was protected, species are repopulating, and the area is now back to its former glory," James says.

Water out, water in

While flood protection will continue to be essential to Deben farmers, so too will the irrigation that has helped to turn their farmland into some of the most productive in the country.

James currently has a licence to use 10 million gallons of water over the summer period, but like other farmers in the area he is interested in a more joined-up approach that captures water currently pumped out into the Deben. "Irrigation has transformed very poor land into very productive land and we have to support that by using resources more efficiently," he says. "If we can make use of some of the run-off, it could help to sustain farms in the area for years."

Karen suggests it could also provide a growing local population with a more reliable and cost-effective water supply. To this end, the Felixstowe Hydro Cycle is aiming to offer a more holistic approach to water management, with a network of pipes designed to distribute collected rainwater between 11 local farms for use during the drier summer months. This would also prevent excess rainwater from discharging into the river and increasing the risk of damaging precious saltmarsh.

Left Kingsfleet, near the mouth of the Deben, where the Felixstowe Hydro Cycle for water management is being developed
Opposite Farmer James Foskett and the now-repaired stretch of river wall fronting a new wetland area, and the restored farm land beyond

'Almost unique' John McCarthy and Dr Helene Burningham (opposite) consider coastal dynamics at the Deben entrance

Changes at the mouth

The Deben has shingle features that are "almost unique throughout the world", according to the coastal scientist Dr Helene Burningham. Strong tides, big waves and huge swathes of shingle are a powerful combination, constantly reshaping the knolls (shingle banks) at the entrance to the river. Coastal defences, climate change and associated sea-level rise are bringing about changes, often dramatic and happening over a short period of time. "These environments are typically complex and the decisions we make that guide their future management need to take account of multiple influences and outcomes," Helene says.

Deben lovers and experts agree that flood risk is among the more pressing issues. "Much of the low-lying agricultural land within the valley was the former floodplain and estuary intertidal zone," says Helene. "Having been disconnected from tidal water for several hundred years, these areas are now below the elevation of the modern saltmarsh and are at significant risk from flooding, placing a lot of pressure on the embankments and fronting marsh to provide the necessary flood defence."

Images on Helene's blog (www.suffolkinlets.wordpress.com) show some of the dramatic changes at the mouth of the river. Flood protection further north is replacing shingle banks with hard defences that inhibit the movement of shingle to the south, which has traditionally

helped to protect the entrance. This raises the possibility of the mouth being exposed to sea-level rise linked, inevitably, to the threat of climate change.

"The dynamics of the Bawdsey and Felixstowe shorelines also impact the Deben estuary through their influence on the mouth of the river, and in particular The Knolls," says Helene. "These undulating banks provide important protection, to Felixstowe Ferry in particular, by forcing waves to break further offshore and reducing their impact on the shorelines of the lower estuary. Sediment moves back and forth through these shoals, but the net direction of movement is southward. This drives the gradual migration of the banks, shifting the channel to run closely around the Felixstowe golf course shoreline until the flow is insufficient, and the tide cuts a new course through the banks closer to Bawdsey, and the whole cycle starts again."

The upshot, as Helene and interest groups like the River Deben Association agree, is that throughout the estuary there is a need for careful and collective decision-making around where and when to intervene in the name of flood protection. "While it is possible to forecast change, the engagement and involvement of people – the Deben community as a whole – is equally important," Helene says.

Safeguard our river

And what of the Deben's future north of Ufford, where it ceases to be tidal? Walking this unspoiled stretch is a peaceful, pastoral experience, from the water meadows around Ufford to the trickles and streams of the nascent river at Easton, Letheringham and Brandeston.

The experts we have spoken to in this book remind us how important it is to preserve the ecology of the Deben and to keep the non-tidal river flowing and clear of debris. Intervene in one part of the waterway and you can impact on another. Tree planting, the clearing of debris and wildlife protection are all measures that help to keep the river alive in its upper reaches.

Channels of communication along the Deben are arguably as strong as they have ever been. Various interest groups and individuals are talking to each other and to those who have the power to implement change. "We are all custodians of the river," says the Woodbridge-based yachtsman Richard Hare. "It's up to us to have our say when we think it's necessary."

"The river is part of our lives," agrees the farmer James Foskett. "I'd be lost if I had to farm somewhere else. We all have to work together to look after what we have." His thoughts are echoed by so many people who value life on the Deben.

As John McCarthy says at the close of the *Life on the Deben* film: "With its hidden depths, the river Deben is truly a charming and magical place. We must all work together to safeguard the future of this wonderful resource."

As pressures grow on the way we live, this book shows how the river can soothe the tensions of modern life. Here is a call for action: let us safeguard the increasingly delicate balance between mankind's needs and those of the natural world that we seek to enjoy, celebrate and preserve for future generations.

Deben resources

Government organisations, agencies, district and local councils, community groups, academics and individuals contribute to the governance and health of the Deben. These include:

The **Deben Estuary Partnership** is a consortium that allows agencies such as the Environment Agency and Natural England, plus local organisations and individuals, to evolve collectively agreed policy and action. Stakeholders represented within the DEP include the National Trust, essentially a landowner with interests in heritage, and the Suffolk Coast & Heaths AONB, which promotes the conservation and enhancement of the legally protected countryside and is keen on the "natural capital" approach to valuing the environment. The East Suffolk Internal Drainage Board, which is responsible for water management across much of the low-lying flood plain, is also represented.
debenestuarypartnership.co.uk

Deben Estuary Pilot, the website of Felixstowe Ferry's harbour master, John White, offers information on navigating the Deben entrance, as well as weather updates and other local intelligence.
debenestuarypilot.co.uk

The **Department for Environment, Food and Rural Affairs** has responsibility for flood and coastal-erosion risk management and provides funding through grants to the Environment Agency and local authorities.
gov.uk/defra

The **Environment Agency** has management and operational responsibility for flooding and coastal erosion, including risk planning, advice to government and developing a framework to support local delivery.
environment-agency.gov.uk

Natural England, the government's adviser for the natural environment in England, has a duty to protect nature and landscapes for people to enjoy.
gov.uk/natural-england

The **River Deben Association** was formed in 1992 as a strong local-interest group to protect the character, beauty and environment of the river. It publishes a magazine of river news for members twice a year.
riverdeben.org

Dr Helene Burningham runs a blog called **Suffolk Inlets**, on which she considers the coastal dynamics affecting the future shape of the river entrance.
www.suffolkinlets.wordpress.com

The **Suffolk Wildlife Trust** is the only organisation dedicated to protecting Suffolk's wildlife and countryside.
suffolkwildlifetrust.org

The **Woodbridge Riverside Trust** has been set up to protect, preserve and enhance the character of the Woodbridge riverside for the benefit of everyone.
woodbridgeriversidetrust.org

The **National Trust's Sutton Hoo** is home to an Anglo-Saxon royal burial ground, Tranmer House and visitor centre.
nationaltrust.org.uk/sutton-hoo

The Tide Mill is Woodbridge's working mill and living museum.
woodbridgetidemill.org.uk

A History of Whisstock's Boatyard
by Sue Whisstock is published by Leiston Pres

Acknowledgements

The authors would like to thank all those patient and thoughtful people who have been involved in the development of this book, specifically:

Malcolm Hodd and Simon Read, who shared their extensive knowledge of the river with information and commentary.

Our editor, Isla McMillan, for her professionalism, guidance and advice.

Chris Bennett, for his help and enthusiasm.

With thanks for insightful interviews and authoritative comments: Joan and Peter Freeman, David Rackham, Cate Meadows, Susan Clark, Dr Sam Newton, Professor Chris Scull, Claudia Myatt, Chris Landt, Ian Maples, Martin and Nedra Pimlott, Alan Fuller, Geoff Sinton, Dan Tarrant-Willis, Clarissa Vincent, Jan Pulsford, Claire Cordeaux, Art Butler, Peter Hepworth, Andrew Osborn, Emma Roodhouse, John Day, Gilbert Sills, Hugh Webster, Annie Turner, Robert Simper, Frances Alexander, Colin Lister, Terry Davey, Jacq Barnard, Jon and Linda Wilkins, Bob Crawley, John Archer, Barry Vincent, Jo and Robert Smellie, Tam Grundy, Carol Reid, Simon Skeet, Penny Hemphill, Simon Rudland, Peter and Mary Wain, John White, Karen Thomas, James Foskett, Helene Burningham and Richard Hare.

The majority of pictures featured in this book are by Tim Curtis, but we would like to thank the following for allowing us to use their special images: Roe Woodroffe, Adrian Green, Jemma Watts, Sue Whisstock, Mike Nunn, Philip Leech, Sutton Hoo Ship's Company, Mercie Lack, the British Museum, Professor Martin Carver and Mary Wain. Thanks also to Shervorn Monaghan for her work on the cover image.

Paintings and illustrations: special thanks to Ipswich Museum and the Suffolk County Council Archaeological Service for allowing us to use their images; thanks also to The Day Collection at the East Anglian Traditional Art Centre for images on pages 76, 77, 79, 80 and 81. The Ramsholt church cottage painting on page 105 is from *A History of Ramsholt* by Ruth Mock.

About the authors

Nick Cottam (pictured above) has been a writer and journalist for more than 30 years. During this time he has written widely for newspapers and magazines, working in a number of fields, including the environment and technology. Nick, who lives in Suffolk, enjoys wildlife and nature and takes every opportunity to walk or run beside his local River Deben.

Tim Curtis is a filmmaker and cameraman who fell in love with the River Deben when he moved to Suffolk 12 years ago. After the huge success of the film *Life on the Deben*, Tim was often asked to produce something else about this ever-popular river. Well, here it is – *Life on the Deben* in print! Tim designed this book, as well as supplying most of the imagery.

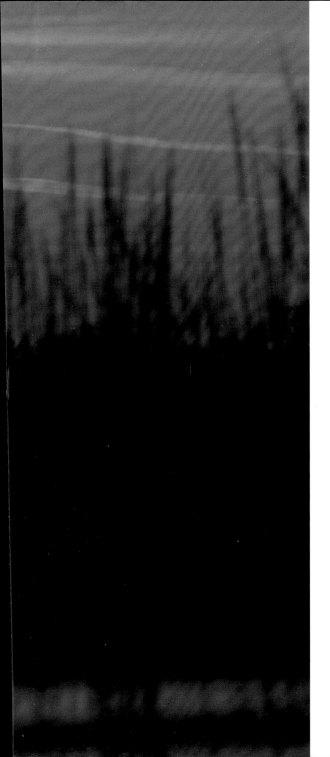

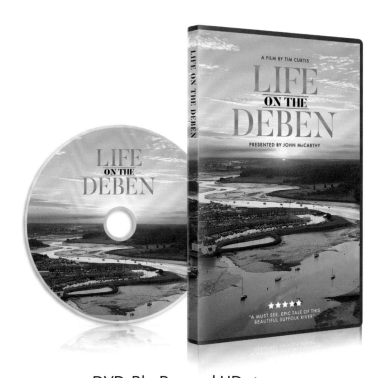

DVD, Blu-Ray and HD stream
available from lifeonthedeben.com